SELECTED POEMS

Theodore Weiss
SELECTED POEMS

TRIQUARTERLY BOOKS
NORTHWESTERN UNIVERSITY PRESS

EVANSTON, ILLINOIS

TriQuarterly Books
Northwestern University Press
Evanston, Illinois 60208-4210

Copyright © 1995 by Theodore Weiss. Published 1995 by
TriQuarterly Books/Northwestern University Press.
All rights reserved. Printed in the United States of America

ISBN   0-8101-5037-9 CLOTH
0-8101-5040-9 PAPER

Library of Congress Cataloging-in-Publication Data

Weiss, Theodore Russell, 1916–
   [Poems. Selections]
   Selected poems / Theodore Weiss.
     p. cm.
   ISBN 0-8101-5037-9. — ISBN 0-8101-5040-9 (pbk.)
   I. Title.
PS3545.E4735A6   1995
811'.54—dc20   95-1841
                           CIP

The paper used in this publication meets the minimum
requirements of the American National Standard for Information
Sciences—Permanence of Paper for Printed Library Materials,
ANSI Z.39-48-1984

CONTENTS

I

FROM

The Catch

«1951»

❖ ✦ ❖

The Hook   3
A Sum of Destructions   5
The Dance Called David   7
After Five Years   10
A Commonplace   12

15

FROM

Outlanders

«1960»

❖ ✦ ❖

Preface   17
Sonata Pathétique   19
A Gothic Tale   20
Barracks Apt. 14   21
A Local Matter   23
The Fire at Alexandria   26
An Egyptian Passage   28
The Giant Yea   30
A Working Day   33
A Trip Through Yucatán   36
House of Fire   37

41

Gunsight

«1962»

85

FROM

The Medium

«1965»

❖ ✦ ❖

The Medium 87
Clothes Maketh the Man 89
A World to Do 90
In the Round 91
Studying French 93
Into Summer 94
On Stuffing a Goose 95

97

FROM

The Last Day and the First

«1968»

❖ ✦ ❖

The Last Day and the First 99
Caliban Remembers 100
A Letter from the Pygmies 121
The Life of . . . 123
Far Out, Far In 125

129
Pasternak and Ivanov:
Translations, Adaptations, Associations
«1968-77»

❖ ✦ ❖

BORIS PASTERNAK

The Breakup   131
Illness   135

SUITE FOR BORIS PASTERNAK

A Russian Lesson   137
Malady   140
November Late   142
"Fresh Paint"   143
Sultry Dawn   144
A Poem Recalled   145
Inside the Storm   146
From A to Z   148
A Summer Thunderstorm   148
Blithewood   150
This Gray Age   150
To Anna Akhmátova   151

GEORGY IVANOV

"Thank god there is no Tsar"   153
"Sleeping, he saw Ophelia in his dream"   154
"The affair was badly flawed"   154
"That pointless happiness, was it worth it?"   155
"Losing yourself in thought, daydreaming"   155
"Mirrors, reflecting each other"   156

157

FROM

The World Before Us
«1970»

❖ ✦ ❖

Pleasure, Pleasure 159
The Heir Apparent 160
"Yes, But . . ." 161
The Youngest Son 163
The Last Letters 165
A Certain Village 167

169

FROM

Fireweeds
«1976»

❖ ✦ ❖

Ten Little Rembrandts 171
Off to Patagonia 172
Another and Another and . . . 174
The Storeroom 175
As You Like It 195
Views & Spectacles 196
Things of the Past 199
A Charm Against the Toothache 200
The Cure 212
The Library Revisited 213
The Late Train 215
Before the Night 216
The Polish Question 217

227

FROM

Views & Spectacles
«1979»

❖ ✦ ❖

The Quarrel   229
The Rapture   230
Autobiographia Illiteraria   231

233

Recoveries
«1982»

289

FROM

A Slow Fuse
«1984»

❖ ✦ ❖

Camel in the Snow   291
Building   292
A Living Room   294
A Slow Fuse   309
A Pair of Shoes   311
The Place of Laughter   312
The Here and Now   313
Making It   315
The Death of Fathers   318
The Hostage   321
Earthrise   322

325
FROM

From Princeton
One Autumn Afternoon
«1987»

❖ ✦ ❖

From Princeton one
autumn afternoon. 1986   327

I   327

II   328

III   328

XXX   329

FROM

The Catch

«1951»

The Hook

I

The students, lost in raucousness,
caught as by the elder Breughel's eye,
we sit in the college store
over sandwiches and coffee, wondering.
She answers eagerly: the place was fine;
sometimes the winds grew very cold,
the snows so deep and wide she lost
sight of people. Yes, she was well
satisfied with her work, expected—
while the quarry's owner was away—
to do another year of it.

II

She is hammering. I hear
the steady sound inside our dry,
noisy days. Sparks fly; the mind,
so taken, mighty for a moment,
becomes quarry and sculptor both,
something caught like love and war
in this golden mesh: and daring
caught that flings like sparks girls
and boys, flagrant cities prompt
to daring's will, love and war
its burly seconds.

III

I see again three kids we passed,
three kids lounging at the edge
of a forsaken quarry like something
they had built; in its sleepy pool
they found the whiteness of their bodies,
the excitement like parian marble.

IV

Such the waters we find ourselves
in. We sit in the college store absorbed
in food and talk. Eagerness seizes us
like love that leaves its best sailors
in the mighty waves, love the word
for hook whose catching, and the struggle
there, is one great musical clash
of minds—each wave a passion and a mind—
a possessed, tumultuous monument
that would be free.

V

                We strain forward
as to some fabulous story. Incandescence
springs from her, the hammer of remembrance
fresh, the young woman, bulky graceful body,
face shining, who sculptured all winter
alone near the source of her rock,
digging down into the difficult rock:

the young woman who lost a day once,
talked to her cat, and when the mirror
of her art became too clear, when dreaming
seemed too big for night alone, took long

‹ 4 ›

walks back to people, back to speech,
and time:
               the woman, who at last—
"I do not use live models"—sculptured fish—
"I remember long lonely holidays at shores
when the spray alone defined green shapes
approaching"—has just seen (her eyes
still gleam with the gleam of it,
blink like the making of many
a take) a great catch.

     VI

                    April, we say,
is the time for fish, for reaching
in its sea-like waftings one
of earth's original conclusions
like the leftover gill slits
the singing student told us about
in this very spot just two days ago . . .

we are in the middle of a great catch,
there collected as from her year-long
lonely rock, the thrashing, clean-
scaled, clear-lit shad in the net.

A Sum of Destructions

The amities of morning
and the buxom habits of birds
that swing a bell-bright city
in their intelligent wings;

last night's squall has
drawn off like anger's tide,
the remote and muffled waters
beating solitudinous rocks

and murmurous
in the hidden parts, ebbing
and beating, of the mind
as some half-forgotten name . . .

the rain has withdrawn
like the tents and the Greeks,
like the hard-to-believe-
in days of our childhood.

Light moves, the whole
massed flotilla of morning, kin
to the upward flight of birds
returning;
   and brutality,
the hungers and the hatreds
seem fabulous, seem members;
the gouty rat and straggly

root collaborate. Earth
in wounds, deaths, decays—
past hours its rutted crusts—
with the billowy sky

is the field-
upon-field, and all one,
of one master observing
the various fruits:
     somewhere
a child in a cage, inferior
bodies making a passable
road, a girl passionate

with pain, an old man
watching the earth escape
like his once endless
strengths, his poems head-

long. And one fills
with awe—as the town
with morning, every cranny,
the birds brimming fire-

escapes and broken windows—
that the earth like some wise
breath never balked, a many-
membered bird-flight,

should include all,
must be a terrible good.
The eyes passing,
contracted from night

and war the stars
undertook, finally emerge
the topgallant of morning,
and those eyes roam

free as the Greeks:
wherever a drop of water
is, spindrift city of water
gleaming, there is home.

The Dance Called David

How could I know
how beyond this love

which held me to him and
by its very hold blinded me?

Hours of many days
we walked, past the reputable,
through scenes, people, past
street-names and corners,
                              deep
through poverty with its charming
air of things half-dropping off
into oblivion.
                    Words from me,
pointings to oddities in color,
sudden, explosive sights
and sounds,
                    recalled him
as those that burned in hell
steadied their flames to answer
one earthbound.
                         Like something
mattered out of air, a smile—
did it reflect the morning
songs that once enlightened?—
would flicker, then go out.

How could I know,
I who loved him, viewed
the world around us as phrases
visible of his unmoving lips,
a music incredible, illuminated
as a battered hurdy-gurdy
by the love he simply woke,

how could I know
how right I was: windows
strewn behind us, swirling

traffic, parks bouqueting lovers,
children burst from school,
all movements in the meaning
mysteriously clear he was for me.

Only now, years after
his death, do I know what
terror I called friend, what
wrestlings I walked beside, what
anguish—dance of madness, gaiety—
he adorned,
            the total city
with its grey wizen streets,
each ash-pale puddle, its thin
furtive faces, and the tiniest
broken straw looked after.

Only now I see
how much he deserved—
if love must deserve—whatever
love I could attain, and more, I
speechless, ignorant as a child.

These years between, now
that he is with what we are not,
time and the multiple wild fears
have helped me recognize what
first must have frightened me
away.
      Time that cut us
off sharper than space can
holds out again generous hands
as he, the harmonious blacksmith,
leads me through the depths unroll-
ing, these scarred years that are
journeying and pity, of myself.

After Five Years

Beside the lumber
recently cut, some men
struggling up a muddy, snow-
ridged road, and five-stories-tall
in your peak-roofed apartment
where warmth was common,

I, after these years
wondrous about returning,
fearful a little,
more than a little hopeful
before the host of possibilities,

I, anxious for revival,
standing at your porthole
window, the latenoon sky
sullen above your sea,
                              ships
puffing along, humped peddlers,
so that I cannot, do not care
to, pursue romantic thoughts
of their cargoes, voyages,
extravagant adventures,

I, a raveled thread
at the needle's eye, asquint
after the flashing pattern
of my silent partners, try hard
to think of you spun back,
gathered into your imagery:

this sky not yet beginning
to ripen your excellent moon,

the mindless sea adrift
with its abstract boats.

And try with disappointment.
For nothing happens, no north
of thunder scours my hearing,
no lightning hallows my thought
or brightens my conscience,

not even this fruit, here
in this bowl as it used to be
promising incredible secrets,
stirs its ruddy lips
to the words of love
and acknowledgement
we somehow always expected;

not the books where we left
them, dusty, close-mouthed
as the phrases we mixed,
sometimes beat into a blow

that swirled this room,
crow's nest, back
to first seas breaking,
furious exultant pain.
                    Only
five nameless unshaped men drag
along the turning, muddy road
next to the new wood, raw,
awkward, an eyesore,
five men for the moment
flickering
            (even as flakes
of snow begin to prick the sky-
light we used to praise,

a god's view, so we said,
for our eyes raised),
                    then
slipping—hardly anguish—
through a narrow break
in the grey fence just below;
                    and they are gone.

A Commonplace

as the silly shepherds
after their first radiant scare—
sheep and cattle at their munching
with the winter
                    bent yet spin-
ning lilies—forgot . . . hunched
puttering over our benighted star,
we lose track of tears.

See him stamped there,
come down into the common-
place who let himself be stabled
in the blood.
                    His walk
brought sea, salt, fish, bread
of his body. Yet within his memory,
each breath travail,

did loiterings of his past,
in sleep perhaps, cajole him: pride,
when as a child he confounded
the learned elders;

                    lust:
touched by a woman long possessed,
he knew his virtue troubled
in him;
            or pain itself, simple-
minded pain, did it perhaps reduce
him to the pulse of immediately
suffering man?
                    O garden
of agony, so dry it drank his blood,
grew in him, till he cried with a man
mouth and a man mortality . . .

but the garden had its malt as well.
For the shepherds, far inland, blood-
warmed, the star faded into a stone
their cattle sucked for salt.

❖ ❖ ◆ ❖ ❖

FROM

Outlanders

«1960»

❖ ❖ ◆ ❖ ❖

Preface

"Sonja Henie," the young girl,
looking out of the evening paper,
cries, "just got married!"

"I don't care if she did,"
the mother replies. "She's been
married before; it's nothing new."

Darnel, Ragweed, Wortle

And turning to me, the young poet
tries to say once more what weeds
mean to him—
                    luscious weeds
        riding high, wholly personal:
        "O go ahead, hack away as much
        as you like; I've been thrown out
        of better places than this"—

his face just come back from staring
out the window into a day
wandering somewhere in early fall
and a long quiet contented rain,

the sky still on his face, the barn
out there, green-roofed and shiny,
gay in a wet way with its red
wet-streaked sides.

‹ 17 ›

                    I read his poem,
mainly about how much it likes weeds,
how definite they are, yet how hard
to come by.
                    I say, "Like all the rest
only their own face will do, each
a star squinting through 30,000 years
of storm for its particular sky."

And as though a dream should try
to recollect its dreamer, we look out
across the long highways of rain,
look out

    Darnel, Ragweed, Wortle

I do not say what we both are thinking
as we see it flicker in that rain-
soaked day: the face exceeding
face, name, and memory,
yet clinging to our thoughts.
                              Black
against the sky, a flock of cranes
shimmers, one unbroken prickly rhythm,
wave on wave, keeping summer jaunty
in its midst.
            And Sonja Henie,
the star, the thin-ice skater,
after many tries, tries once more.

"The poem's not right. I know,
though I worked at it again and again,
I didn't get those old weeds through.
I'm not satisfied, but I'm not done
            with it yet."

There in that wheatfield
of failures, beside all manner
of barns, frost already experimenting,
the slant of weather definitely
fall, lovely scratchy

Darnel, Ragweed, Wortle

Sonata Pathétique

Let it be some sheets of music,
molding lamplight into the shapes
of music, and a fly, a last
survivor in this bleak November,
cross-legged on the page, humming
to itself like one of the black
notes come alive.
     I listen
as though to overhear the strains
of a great green air it once
belonged to, archaic chord. Yet
flicking shabby wings that sparkle
in the haloing light, it sings
no plaintive tune.
     Ah, fly,
about your composition what can
I say? But moments there are
undoubtedly so self-willed, self-
fulfilling, that the day of their
emerging glitters, little more
than grit upon their wings.

                              Then
they, outlandish, zither about
until they find some setting—
sheets of music in a lamplight—
they can be moderately at home in.
But one there was, old weather-
beat, much noted
                    for his feats,
like you a lone survivor, and what-
ever the measures meted out
to him, a dapper dancer, by his
clever footwork never too far
from his true estate . . . a scurry,
and you are purring in our cat.

A Gothic Tale

Framed by our window, skaters, winding
in and out the wind, as water reeling
so kept in motion, on a well-honed
edge spin out a gilded ceiling.

Fish, reflecting glow for glow,
saints around the sun, are frozen
with amazement just one pane below.

Skates flash like stars, so madly
whirling one can hardly tell which
is sky and which the watery floor . . .

one night two straitlaced couples,
a footman over them, rode out

in a dappled-horse-drawn sleigh
onto the river, a moonlit lark.

The ice broke and they—sleigh,
footman and all—riding in state,
rode straight on into the lidded water.

That winter all winter folks twirled
over them who—framed in lace,
frost the furs, the shiny harness
and their smiles the fire that keeps
the place—sat benignly watching.

"One foot out, one foot in,
are we real," thought one, "we who
wander sheepishly in dreams, or they,
the really sleepless eyes, under us?

And every night who knows (a laughter
troubles us like dreams) who skates
(a thousand watch fires the stars)
above, peering through the pane?"

Barracks Apt. 14

All must be used:

this clay whisky jug, bearing
a lampshade; the four brown pears,
lying ruggedly among each other
in the wicker basket; the cactus
in its pot; and the orange berries,

old now, dangled from their twigs
as though badly hung there.

Like the picture lopsided
on the wall, stalks wrangling
in a peevish wind, yet the crows
flapping out a harmony all their own.

These as well as the silence,
the young woman reading Aristotle
with difficulty, and the little girl
in the next room, voluble in bed:
"I'm talking in my sleep . . . laughing
in my sleep . . . waking in my sleep,"

all are parts hopeful, possible,
expecting their place in the song;
more appealing because parts
that must harmonize into something
that rewards them for being, rewards
with what they are.
                        Do this and do,
till suddenly the scampering field
you would catch, the shiny crows
just out of reach, the pears
through which a brown tide breaks,
and the cactus you cannot cling to
long like that thorny Aristotle
suddenly, turning,
                        turn on you
as meaning, the ultimate greenness
they have all the time been seeking
in the very flight they held
before you.
                        No matter what you do,

at last you will be overwhelmed,
the distance will be broken,

the music will confound you.

A Local Matter

I

But who does us?
Who flexes like fingers, strains
in our sinews that they sing,
one felicitous agony?
These thoughts, these thoughts
thieving through night that things—
even hope and lust everlastingly
raucous—heckling locals
trying to distract us,
fall dumb.

II

The cat all evening
lulled the mouse, licked it
and pricked it and loved it that
never a moment did it move
out of sight. O the success,
the bliss, the fittingness
of nature there; mouse
recognized its consummation, its all-
devoted, all-devouring heir,

where the future was
suddenly breathless.
Grin, claws.

III

Hum of mouths within me:
waters at their loom spinning
out the sea, the lilies
in their velvet skill break
stones, break stems for a somewhere-
rooted, roar-cored wind.

IV

And you, enchanting
the maddest din as winter
pears can pipe the speckled curves
in scented air of summer round,
do you not, like that lady
of the wild things, discover
in your bending
wells, a company of drinkers
borne up by the swell?

V

These the lines
I do not somehow have
to learn; they find their parts
at the moment of burning:
the appropriate pain, the fitting
grief. Meantime I cling
to things that belong:
shag-root of a dog
not the whole world can impress,

the sparrow tucked in the sky
ticking out fall.

VI

And yet the subtle
strings twang into us all;
I think of turtles in a bowl,
their shells like painted shields,
churning upon one another,
each overwrought by private music,
rushing together to one
gleaming doom.

VII

Now in the lute-time,
soon brute, of the year I
slouch down, the silky lounge
of one in perfect health
(hear the chestnut
gayly crying in its country fire).
I lounge as I wait the advent
of one all sinew and strain,
the lunge. Like a string tautening
to the discords of precisianist
pain, I fit: come, windy
dark, like all the kingdoms
of the North and within the gates
of my Jerusalem set your serried
singing thrones!

VIII

In the state of weeds,
high-spirited undergrowth,

‹ 25 ›

there congregate vast dynasties.
Themselves flashing armor and plume
before the shadow coming on
of the long summer light, locusts
clash their cymbals.
Again and again, mighty in leaves
as Nimrod, the mouse enters
that the seasons be maintained
as locally as a broken fence
beside a yawning dog,

IX

till I, skinned,
glistening, one of many
hides racked in a row, lesser
tale in a larger, from the lean-
to of noon, sink to mouse, catgut,
fiddlings of some nameless bog.
At work religiously, maggots welcome
me passing through, goodwill
from one end of death to the other,
into and through that minerals
know me, the odors use me;
how the hum becomes me,
once and ever the household
word of the air.

The Fire at Alexandria

Imagine it, a Sophocles complete,
the lost epic of Homer, including no doubt

his notes, his journals, and his observations
on blindness. But what occupies me most,
with the greatest hurt of grandeur, are those
magnificent authors, kept in scholarly rows,
whose names we have no passing record of:
scrolls unrolling Aphrodite like Cleopatra
bundled in a rug, the spoils of love.

Crated masterpieces on the wharf,
and never opened, somehow started first.
And then, as though by imitation, the library
took. One book seemed to inspire another,
to remind it of the flame enclosed
within its papyrus like a drowsy torch.
The fire, roused perhaps by what it read,
its reedy song, raged Dionysian, a band
of Corybantes, down the halls now headlong.

The scribes, despite the volumes wept
unable to douse the witty conflagration—
spicy too as Sappho, coiling, melted
with her girls: the Nile no less, reflecting,
burned—saw splendor fled, a day consummate
in twilit ardencies. Troy at its climax
(towers finally topless) could not have been
more awesome, not though the aromatic house
of Priam mortised the passionate moment.

Now whenever I look into a flame,
I try to catch a single countenance:
Cleopatra, winking out from every spark;
Tiresias eye to eye; a magnitude, long lost,
restored to the sky and the stars he once
struck unsuspected parts of into words.
Fire, and I see them resurrected,
madly crackling perfect birds, the world

lit up as by a golden school, the flashings
of the fathoms of set eyes.

An Egyptian Passage

Beside me she sat, hand hooked and hovering,
nose sharp under black-lacquered hair,
and body, skinny, curving over a brownish big
thick book.
        I glanced past her hand to pages
she checked; there, beside strange symbols,
curious hawk-beaked little birds at attention,
gawky beasts, stiff plants, which I, despite
rail-shuttling shadows and battering light
at the end of tunnels, gradually made out
as items in a German-Egyptian lexicon.

Then red- and black-brick tenements; billboards;
excavations; three boys with mattocks, digging
by a squat, half-finished, bushy hut;
tumbled-together shacks, drifting in the way
of winter; smokestacks; near the bank,
its wharf rotted through in several places,
a gutted house like something done by fire,
slowly floating (so it seemed) out on the river;

and the dumps, one burning in three spots,
lurid like old passion among heavy, piled-
up boxes and black, banged-in pots, and birds
floating above like ashes.
        Birds too
on the Hudson: ducks in strict formation,

gulls—like lungs—working their great wings
or perched like dirty, jagged lumps of ice
on the ice caking the shoreward waters.
And all fashion of ice, from shoots in spray
to zigzag rows, waves at their apex trapped.

Along the shore a shaggy, red-brown brush,
so thick partridges must be crouching in it,
as in the Hudson, under an icy lid,
a brood of clouds. And heavy-headed, long,
thin, flaggy things like the stuff we think of
growing by the Nile.
                  The trees across the river
rigid, bare, through them the early light
already deepened, purpling. As through
the little crate-white houses, quiet enough,
but indoors, I knew, no bush for its morning
birds busier.
            Still her eyes never left
the ibises that fluttered under her fingers.
Deeper and deeper she went, like the sun
unfolding fields, forsaken spots, and towns,
the dirty sharp details of, always more
and always clearer—like the river itself,
the roads agog with golden high-legged going,
song-sparrows swept from their nests, their wings
praising the sun—the steeples, broken houses
and smoky streets, kids dashing in and out
of hide-and-seek, the billowy wash on lines.

And I thought of sitting on a polar star
a million miles away, looking down at this earth
surrounded by its tiny nimbus of a day.
And I saw the days—each hour a speck, twelve
motes combined—like waves like sparks like bushes
burning, lined up one by one, for its intricate

strokes each a kind of word.
                    "Poughkeepsie,"
the conductor said as he took her ticket
from the seat. Several times he tapped her
on the shoulder before she looked up, fumbled
for her coat and bag, and lurched out.

The Giant Yea

. . . who can bear the idea of Eternal Recurrence?

    I

Even as you went over, Nietzsche,
in your last letter, as ever, you tried
to reach him:
                    "Dear Herr Professor,
When it comes to it I too would very much
prefer a professorial chair in Basel
to being God; but I did not dare to go
so far in my private egoism as to refrain
for its sake from the creation of the world."

The past before him, the hateful present
stifling no end of futures with noisy smoke,
what could the Dear Herr Professor, magnificently
sober Jacob Burckhardt, do or do for you;
how thrust pitiful hands into what proclaimed
itself a sacred solitude?
                    Maybe too at times,
syringa blowing through his classroom (gape-
mouthed angels Paracelsus pressed into his lectures
in this very room, throwing all Basel

‹ 30 ›

into an uproar and a hatred that finally
drove him out,
            familiars also like a rout
of mornings bickering to swell the retinue
of Dr. Faustus after breakfast), trumpeting
through the profundity of his pauses,

maybe he could let that host, with nothing
to lose in being, be themselves, especially
as there sprang among them heroes out of Raphael
with everything to gain.
            Even now Astorre
the horseman, in the twinkle of that scholar
eye, spurs quarrying the dark, falcon-plumed,
plunges, a warrior of Heaven, to the rescue
of a youth, fallen with copious wounds,
by this aid exalted.

    II

            Alas, for all Astorre's
audacious charging down the margin of the page,
the Professor's age, parading with its Sunday
family-walks and the thundrous drummers of Basel
in trim, upholstered parks, benumbed him.

What was there for him to do who saw
his begetters, fighting men, furious, mighty
in their pride, tumbled to such petty end?

That beauty being slain on the high places
in the midst of its noblest battle, should he,
exclaiming, dare to tell it, publish it
in the streets so prim and polished, to see
the daughters of the philistines rejoice?

He let you go, best emparadised,
or so you said, in the sparkling shadow
of a sword, retiring into frozen heights,
a terrible loneliness, enhanced by sun.

III

At the end, rocks breaking their doors for you,
out poured the shaggy men, hordes of flame
and drunkenness. Solitude, dressed in winds
and falcons, rang, a honeycomb of voices
hailing:
    dancer David; Agamemnon, amethyst
with proud and deadly twisting; Dr. Faustus;
Borgia and Astorre, those human hours,
sowing splendors with their wily wrists.

The peaks, much moved, conscious of the love
that guides by the same capricious path as stars
the agony, the maggot's tooth, hurtling
to your beloved town, stormed its arcades
past the drowsiest beds. God was dead,
long live the gods.
     In that third-floor room,
still going about in your academic jacket
and down at heel, all the heavens rejoicing,
laughing, lifting up your legs,
into the middle of the rout you leaped,
a satyr's dance, as always, the conclusion
of the tragic truth . . .

IV

      You in what we are,
alas, and by your effort that had to fail
have reached us.

And we go, perhaps as the Dear
Herr Professor did, saddened that we cannot
give ourselves,
        the Greeks at last, Paul,
St. Augustine, Luther, Calvin too, surpassed
by the resolution—not time could tame it,
not the mob's indifference—of your fury.

A Working Day

After such a day, too cluttered
for clearing and no way out, no way
to grasp this nameless yet pervasive woe,
after such a day turn to *Genesis:*

ponder the sea before the waves began,
ponder bdellium and the onyx stone
(gold of that land is good), the beasts
got of man's solitude, till woman,
aspiration of his breast, is made. One
flesh, time loitering there.
                    Then "Cursed
is the ground for thy sake." The taste
of the brow's sweat mixed with stubborn
bread this Book knows too well;
the fidgets in ourselves
luxuriate, deft creatures of despair.

Not even the flaming cherubim
could hold that garden in, the snaky weeds
and cankers, plotting and complotting,
avid for this their holiday.

I

You thought,
Thoreau, to sit it out while your giddy
trivial Nineteenth Century preened itself
to death.
          For a time, like a halcyon
perched on a spray, and only a few steps
between you and Concord, you settled in Walden—
long as the season of need prevailed;
your land's lord, you sat it out, secure
the valors you had witnessed, flight
of the seasons, daily in their several lights
remitting more clearly your singular truth.

Then, bold saunterer of morning, gaze fixed
forever on a fresher, greener time, back again,
more private than before.

II

We, in a wood,
dark, cluttered, just outside your field,
admit by the radiance of what you discovered
there, the order of beans in a row,
the sweetness of your clearing, the blight
of this we wished for: piper, pigweed,
Roman wormwood?
               No name can cast a slowing
spell upon that ragtag army, backed
as much as we by sun and rain. We run
through our assets, friends and events,
the whole summer store.
                 No one, no thing
can help us. Least of all those who suffered,
tried grief and terror to what seemed their end.

We think, incredulously, of our first glossy
learning, our pride: not one of the past,
the great we assumed we could lean on
forever, has a word for this.

The day, slowly, like a blind idiot
picking in a rock-pit he thinks garden,
passes us by.

III

                    But you, Henry,
sitting there, going your own way—free
in a world of your own choosing, verge
like that vigorous bean crop between wild
and cultivated fields—were you out of it?

Those companions, mind and body, the populated
self you turned to, unctuous creatures bent
on their own careers, were they to be trusted
any more than the rest?
                    The rift
that should have made us whole, imperfect
from the start, multiplied first loneliness.
One flesh. At the end, foundering in the blood,
you sat it out, watching the inroads
of the darkening wood.

A Trip through Yucatán

You have, in a sense,
been through it all; each experience
has known you, like a Swiss clock
in the middle of the room, forcing
all things to its rickety breathing.

Abruptly then the one out
that you see—rather than swinging
in and out, forever, on a crazy
and precarious stick, pretending
to be another hour, another place,

one of you for one time, another
for the next, and never meeting—
the one out is a breakdown.
Then all things can, with a sigh,
forget you . . .
                        yet after days
of snow, too swiftly falling to be
accounted for, in the middle of it
a moon appears, absurdly beautiful
and warm . . .
                        like the dinner-
party you have just come from where
the speaker assured you your French
accent reminded him of his trip
through Yucatán:
                        a group
of Americans, a few Spaniards,
and several French, all insisting
they understood each other's speech;
only he, interpreting, knew the truth.

Madly, the epitome of tact,
he hopped about from one to the next,
trying to keep their ignorances
from them . . . I have stopped jumping;
and moon-wise, in a sense, arises

that last, implacable light-
heartedness, like emerging mid-jungle
into a jubilant calm, a clearing
of florid birds and plumaged flowers
that set the feastday of the storm.

House of Fire

I

To burn is surely bad, to be
possessed by greed or lust or anger . . .

Down the pathway pebbles clatter
into brush more ashen than the rocks
that mount the cliff; beyond it windows,
flaring, flood the light through vines,
entangled with the thudding wind,
as litter, crackled underfoot, puffs
up the dust of countless little deaths.

And yet in the abandoned field
below, through this intense decaying

and its acrid breath, a freshness wells
as if an April, some forgotten day of,
starting up out of the time's debris,
look round amazedly.

II

                    The man
Job squats among the soot and ashes,
his complaints mingling with the smoke.
He sifts with peeling fingers cinders
of that once his boundless joy:

sheep, camels, oxen and she-asses;
seven sons, three comely daughters,
the tender dewy branch unceasing who
guaranteed the generations of his name
as of his various unique features;
and his fame gone through the streets
a bounteous morning to proclaim him—

        these sift, soft flakes, breaking
            in the flurry of his cries.

III

Yet what lust or greed or anger,
what burning in this house of fire
beyond what becomes a man, that man
who girt up his loins according
to the Lord's command?
                        And sifting
flakes, he strews them in a drunkenness
of despair about his head, the last
fruits of his efforts, the folly
of all living.

‹ 38 ›

Surrender all,
the Whirlwind says, whatever endeared
you even as it made Me dear to you.

No less lovely than the first arriving
leaves at falling; through the nakedness
the mighty music, unmitigated, enters.

Dew all night an ice upon the branch,
the cedars cleaving in the wind,
like a huge flock gathering
in the boughs, each tree achieves
its height the moment when it crashes.

IV

And yet that leveling Wind
did He not summon as witnesses
His freckled, much-loved creatures,
numberless as leaves, yet loved
for individual, self-willed features?

Mane flamboyant, hoof and nostril
bristlings of the mine of fire,
the horse that, leaping forth, saith "Aha!"
no less to battle than to pelting hail;
Leviathan grown tender, weltering
out his rage, the boiling ocean docile
in waves self-absorbed—
                              these, springing
like the hurricane, soft cooing words
around His lips, from God's own fingertips,
warm with them He warms, exult Him surely
in the grandeur and unique particulars
of their pride.

V

Sky and earth
are held in a twilight's rushing
furious fire, earth and sky the route
of pawing hoofs, till all the colors drain
into one conflagration.
But here
as I pause on the little wooden bridge,
the waters, shielded by two arching pines,
needles heaped below, purl into a cat's paw.

Coolly the ripples from one side,
pursuing their dappled course, are crossed
like a shuttle by ripples from the other
till they pour together—yet still
themselves—in the next step
of their streaming.

VI

And so the sea
is fed, and so the fire, the rampant waves
and flames flared up in stubborn homage
to their fathering first desire.

‹ 40 ›

Gunsight

«1962»

Gunsight

(An interior monologue that records, through the voices in him, the sensations and memories of a wounded soldier undergoing surgery.)

Squinting after morning, like a sentry
on a mountaintop, you lie. The hospital
sheets bank round you, drifted as your sleep.
And midnight, come and gone, ghostly in swaddling
snow remains.
    You wait who would be one
with the flowerbed, stretched out in the court
below, one with your leg, a frozen block;
summer it mocks, bundled in that vase,
the roses choking in the oppressiveness
of their own breath.
    By such route morning comes?
Now lies, flight fettered in the ice, wedged
against the pane, as though a pulse throbbed there.
And somewhere, hiding a few stubbed wings, your Robin-
Hooded Wood, leaves fallen like the fairy
tales you stormed through, fumbles in the wind
for berries, fuzzy low faces you once picked,
oozing from your fingertips.

❖ ✦ ❖

    Yet lie here
stony as you will, time, unabated, whirls,
its stars more wily than the dark's snowflakes,

inside your flesh.
                    Even as you drowse
the corridor starts up its echoing.
Morning blue-lipped on her rattling tray,
she, white-breast, black-capped, -winged and -clawed,
arrives. That gimlet look, how far it's come,
like something out of snow. Bent over you,
snow peering into snow, arch, starched,
stiffest nun she is.
                    Be quiet, she says.
Quiet to heal this feverishness? Scraps
of peace, placid nights, best baiting, rouse it,
greedier as it feeds.

                              ✧ ✦ ✧

                    Needle-plunged,
the room begins to rock. A January
hillock knees, unblinking snow claws up.
Down corridor's funnel on a swooping knuckled
cloud, the suck and buffet of the sea.
Doors worked by whisper's hissing draft
swivel you to a crackling wilderness
of lights, explosive glare a gash of knives,
one vast black-lacquered eye.
                              Snowy masks
bent over you, voices flaking, falling,
falling, through the seasick smell

                              breath in

It's cold. Faces, walls fling up at you,
cavernous waves, snow-kneading hands.
Oh fie, that smell

breath in

    deep
past breathing, stench of bodies rotting.

Distance, many-hooded, sidles in.
A mountain stoops. How far it's come!

Through the crack shapes, muffled, flickering,

Can't breathe!

    For crying out loud, cut the shaking.
Want to wake the whole damn wood?

          ◇ ◆ ◇

    Voices,
billowed up and down the air, prickle
everywhere.

    It's only sticky cobwebs,
twigs wrapped in mist. You got the gun.
You said you wanted to hunt.

    Something, skittering,
flaps against your mouth.

    The dawn wind blowing
up—will you look at that lake skedaddle!
Don't be a scaredy-cat, a momma's boy,
scrounge down; keep your eye on that crack.

There in the trees like morning, dew on them,

sparrows by the trillions,

                    squabbling,
the dew's own shrillness,

                 and a giant one,
the sun,

          see that in its beak?

                Wings spout.

Now's the time. Charge!

              Summer pitching
in its leaves, the wood a wilderness of lights,
of one bird zooming through another's flight,

what are you waiting for? Shoot! Shoot!

bullets ricochet—the flock like hurtling
stones—against each rock, each tree.
                     East,
west, the breaking lake, its waters lashed
to wings, all, echoing, roar.
               Across the gunset
heavens redbreast day is falling, flushed
and falling,
       body through which morning sang.

❖ ✦ ❖

Only a handful, take it.

        It's still warm

(come, my love, and lie with me)

still struggling in your hands.

                                        You wanted it,
now *it's all yours.*

                          Breathless, July storming
the mouth

           (we'll lip to lip in mastery
enlarge the airs our senses sing,
the hanging gardens fingers bring)

and through the heart the heartless sea,
oozings from the fingertips,
                        that eye,
that glaring eye,
             won't close.

                          You can't
get rid of it like that.

                    Still it stares
through feathers twirling, tumbled over drifts

(the hills and valleys
hovering, the seas of love)

                    down slippery
peaks to their blooming summit time . . . lolled
on a herd-browsed cloud of clover,

                    Laura!

❖ ✦ ❖

(Inside this spinning bed we rove,
delve into every treasure trove.)

From her hands and mouth it swells

                                     (In coiling
warmth we lie that love, untoiling,
forage in us, finding, share
its raptures in our blended air.)

Exultant, love, the looter, slams its waves
through you.

                (Our honey-suckled kiss
plucking us, we blithely crest
the tide; like a sprig in the beak
of a dove we, soaring, wake)

                        to fall
head over heels

              (into the clover)
closing round.

              (Roses ring us, sweet sighs
mixed with ours.)

              Roses by a field, choking
on their breath and on the wrangling smells,
shit, groans, the rattled gaspings
on the ground,
              her hair alive, hissing,
twisting, rush of wings,

              (that glaring
rigid through your eyes!)

                    The trees loop over,
tangled limbs, lips, cries . . .

                         ❖ ✦ ❖

                              reeling,
caterwauling, night hauling you to rocky
port, the sailors weave you in as they
are woven round with heaving breasts
and rouge-fixed faces,

                         Birdie, Gertie,
Madge and Meg,

                    making light of midnight
stark, mouths like wounds,

                         she wiggles,
hot stuff, sizzling on a spit,

                         sinuous
smoke, twigged and shagged with ice,
hands looking after, horror
in such white hands;
                         and slyly winking
from your polished shoes as on the needle
in and out the olive drab, crookback
of the journey, tracked through cloth
like thread; its knotting torments.

                         ❖ ✦ ❖

Swept out in a reef of faces,
                         Mother

weeping, Father frowning, preacher, teacher,
foamy with questions

> *(say, how many feathers*
on a ruffled breast? its songs, its load
of flights, where do they rest?)

> Shore recoils,
dawn shipwrecked in the toppling clouds,
the breakers of a handkerchief, the cry
spun out into the heave and tumble of the sea.

The black ship, drenched with slops, tosses round
in sleep that mumbles, tide-like, over them;
the sea itself gliding, ghostly dreams,
below, a thousand men smuggle the spoils
of continents,

> *souvenirs brought*
for Birdie, Gertie, Madge and Meg,

triggers clicking; helmets; like a lidless
eye the ruby Joe hacked off a finger for;
and tight-packed voices, babbling lucid
as these waves,

> *snug in our packs*
with brush and comb, tooth by jowl
with Gertie snapt, the spicy note,

they try to read between the scribbled lines
as in the sea; time billows to a white
unbroken, daze like drifting mountainous
snow . . .

❖ ✦ ❖

‹ 50 ›

    weeks on weeks of olive-drab waiting:
dumped in a crummy town, a game's loose cards,
the crumpled dreams, the tattered jokes,
the hands stuck like a clock's.
         Over the barracks
sparrows flying, sun reaped in their wings
as in the trumpets of the tootling band.
And by the drill shed, never breaking ranks,

soldiers, fall in; count off; now cock your rifles,
aim and . . .

     flocks on flocks, dragging the world
away, a great wind blowing up behind,
round and round the company goes, shuffling
a million miles in one small khaki circle,
while dance fumbles after limbs, the pinup
slumped to rutted eyes,

       come on,
boy, it don't mean a thing
if you ain't got that swing,

       legs cast up
and away in the jig of war, the reedy piper,
death, blows through the lusts, the memories,
you and the rest lice sizzling on a leaf
in the wind's lull,

      aw, I'm stuffed to the gizzard
with shave, shit and shinola. A roll in the grass,
that's what I'm for, the water far below
a bare-assed shimmy

      (we crest the tide,
high on a jaunty worldwide
sprig in a bird's beak)

> sweeping back and forth,
billowy heat . . .

❖ ◆ ❖

> *two-bit sweating Anacapri,*
a morning long, a leaf. Sun sashays in
and poppies razzle-dazz under its feet,
grapes, plums and dames panting to be plucked.
This is where July shacks up.

> The town,
dangling from its mountain slope, a fleece,

it's a sheep's life all right, stinks like a goat;
but you got to admit the flock, flooding
down the hill, is flashing in the sun,

its backside in a clump of olives, teeters
on three lopsided streets,

> *wash smacking out—*
and what a sail, a whale, a zeppelin maybe—
the baggy drawers of Poppa Zookie. His cheeks
popt with grins like fish flopping in
a net, the town, its kids and dogs, yipping
at his heels, he grabs us with his smoochy kisses.

And down below, splashing up,

> *the fat-assed*
washerwomen,

> blue-backed, sun-whacked waves.

Smack them as you drink this vino, singing
O Sole Mio, sun blinking boozy through.

◇ ✦ ◇

Now summer gluts, July hunched down,
relentless with its whorish herd of never-
closing blooms, its gasping days, the sunlight
raspy with the muck it's lapping, turning
into dust.
          Dust everywhere: those old men,
squatting by the cemetery wall,
the world, its past, deadweight upon their backs,
like ghosts of ghosts wheeze up their ancestors.

Go digging down inside your dust, one poke
you're through.

          The pebbles crunching underfoot
are bones; in moldy crusts, in cheese each munches
on the dead, wine gurgling down the throat
their guttural blood.

          You think your town's so hot?
Smoky coal-and-iron dump, day and night
it vomits crap on everything. In these
old boys still many a jig is kicking up,
twisting through the dirt.

          Twisted
bits of women, broken from the start,
these ancient wraiths, heads bent together, sigh—
black shawls like shrouds—through fingers,
bony needles in the middle of their web.

Their keening and that steady low-down roar,
the hordes complaining in a too small bed,
a voice, the past's, more nettling than war.

❖ ◆ ❖

Grab the jug. A couple more steps up the hill
and, there, you're out of it. The wine,
the babes, that's the lake to dive into.

The knoll waiting, knees bent for an outing,
the war folded away in the light, a dog-
eared history book to prop the table, folded
away like paper ruins, the calendar
of shattered days and nights ript out,
of scattered cities dropt, the countless lives . . .

❖ ◆ ❖

the nine lined up,
　　　　the dunces,
　　　　　　faces
to the board at the teacher's order,

　　　　　　　　order!
Chalky days remote, humdrum as school,

secure as home, no bug snugger
in its grassy summer,

　　　　　home? its stances
and pretences . . .

　　　　your Father can sit still,
hours on the stoop carving a peg leg

‹ 54 ›

*for that chick. But what time does
he have for us?*

          *(That's the boat, Son,
I promised you. Take this paper, fold it
here and here, it's ready to be launched
to dare whatever waves the Creek can blow.)*

Listen to your Mother; don't go near the water.

(Puff a mouthful, off it scoots.)

          *Phew!
A cargo of your Father's pheasants, pigeons,
cuckoo Noah's ark.*

          *(Trust it, Son;
speedier than any line you draw,
McCreedy's Creek whips you into the Bay
of Biscay, Venice, and the open sea
where the West Indies dance like spicy leaves
upon a tree.
        That bobbing isle's the hideout
for the likes of me,
          old Captain Kidd.
But first we got to shoot*

          *(no time, supplies,
for prisoners, soldiers, line them up,*

*the nine . . .
        the dunces, faces to the wall . . .)*

bang, bang, bang

        (tangled limbs,

lips, cries . . .)

      shove them off the deck
and hurry up; the shore, the morning's
just a step.
      Now jump!

        It's too rocky
to land, too deep and dark.

        You got the bird,
a gold leaf in its beak, to wing you to that
sacred spot: treasure buried where
a limb sticks out.
      My wooden leg'll stamp;
earth rattles and they pop.
        (Watch it! Pigface
Sarge
    old Pontius Preacher
        Teacher
          is bearing
down on you . . .)

⬥ ✦ ⬥

      Teacher scrawls a curve
upon the board and, Columbus gayly bobbing,
it is Spain, refuge of the dawn,
its winter gardens blossoming; another
wriggling stroke
      (like Pocahontas Susie's
pigtails, black and snaky, and her shaky
two-way jiggle as her garter, smacking,
sends you, sends.
      Now snap it.)

                              Something's breaking
loose!

    (only a flock of quail, Son,
winter white-hot, nipping, at their tails)

The world whips by like smoke and crumpled papers
from a train, scraps of cities, distance,
stuck to it, the crazy seasons wrangling.
And your country, spooky in the sun
with highways: miles and miles of no one, nowhere,

(better stay where you belong, Son, holding
on to what's your own,)

                         secure as home,
humdrum as school! That's not the rule you learned.
Even as you pledge allegiance

                              to trickery

in the cloakroom

                    whatever's clutched
soon snatches out of hand.

                    A face looms over?

                    ❖ ✦ ❖

Out of dirty books and bodies—lice sizzling
on a leaf in a wind's lull—the Facts,
acrid with their beetling look, the chalk

who dared to scribble that nasty word across
the board?

‹ 57 ›

                    sour old teacher stinks, ink
and droning voices, sex and summer hum,
as through the barred-off window you are brightest
scholar of, remote in daylight swarming,
Gooseberry Hill lifts its violet text,
then tips, like birds wing-propt, rippling twilight—

Susie's eyes that wink at what she's thinking—

and into the woods it dives of crow-quilled words,
dumb now like dizzy numbers rubbed off the board,
erasers beating, puffed into a cloud
of chalk, into the dark and into the stars
as valentines are cheating in the desk.

                         ✧ ✦ ✧

There in the empty cloakroom the Milkman's Son

I'm an old cowhand

                              is skillfully working over
the pearl-and-ruby, eighteen-carat movements
of the Jeweler's well-set Daughter.

                              Get her
in a corner: you got a hell of a lot
of catching up to do.

                    (In one second
I will teach you more than ten Dogfaces
can in a million books and a trillion years.)

Use this map, the pieces like a jigsaw
fit. That's the clue. You're getting hot.
The answer, treasure, 's at the end of that.

                    ‹ 58 ›

It's Love, LOVE, L O V E makes the world go round.
Get into the spin, boy, be jet-propelled.
Here are the curves, boy, from which to spill.
Here are the swerves, quick trip to the moon,
He who won't take it's an ass-faced baboon.
So come on, boy, kick your feet off the ground.
It's Love, LOVE, L O V E makes the world go round.

(Just like your father, borne by every breeze.)

◇ ◆ ◇

Her garter, snapping, starts a swell that rams
the air—a gap in nature—people popping.
Smoke and snowflakes craze the sky. An engine
batters on the tracks, its lonely nightmare
whistle shrieking, moaning. Midnight slouches
down the street.

> *(Or is it morning, stiff*
and glazed,
> *the crack,*
> *the narrow crack*
where day and darkness meet?)

The recess
crams with yelling Polish kids.

PHEEEEEEEEEUW! There he goes
Momma's boy, Momma's boy
pants like a hog,
grunts like a frog,
can't turn around cause
he's stuck in a bog.

Mid-winter
dark, a thousand corners crouching, keeping
terror bright, a genius, it, coiling,
leaps.
Run!

Scaredy-cat, scaredy-cat . . .

the cold

deep past breathing

is ripping through. Slopes
sliding under you, you stumble,
fall,
roll
like a snowman
round and round
through drifts
to their blooming summit time. Everywhere
a peak frosting your roof, snow-lapped, earth-
lugged, leaf-snug berries, tangy through, the oozing
fingers of Gooseberry Hill . . .

❖ ◆ ❖

O.K.,
boy, grab that bucket and let's go.
Susie, you come too. We'll pick the big
fat berries on the way,

through
these thorny bushes, over these rocks,
these rocks
and rills, round templed hills: high time you learned

‹ 60 ›

a thing or two.
                    Hunch down. Clutch
the hillside, kid; you're Jack in the Beanstalk.
And by the maple, trying out the seasons,
sweaty summer red-faced at the fence,
when you reach the hilltop

                              it's muddy here
and Mother

                    (listen to your Father: you
can trust me; be a man, Son)

                         your turn's next.
I'll warm things up. While we plan out maneuvers
in the barn, you play soldier.
And like a sentinel stick to your post;
anyone who sleeps or runs away
is traitor and must die

                    (must die and die
and die)

          if someone comes you know the signal

her garter smacks

                    (count off, cock your rifles:
get ready, get set)

               march

                    (then we drill
and drill till trees salute and birds—the redcoats
are coming, beware, beware!—stand at attention
mid-air)

‹ 61 ›

❖ ✦ ❖

see that white inside the door,
that gasping through the straw, the tickled cry?
Those hands reaching out,

horror in such white hands!

(twigs and sticky cobwebs . . .)
                              come on, scaredy-
cat, now's your chance. I fixed it . . .

(charge!)

Fee, Fie, Fo, Fum,

(the signal)

thrashing in the strawy dark?

I smell

Oh fie, fie!

the rutted sweat, the blood

Father, Mother!

(What's eating you? You got away.
It's only your own tracks hotfooting after.
Now, still oozing bloody from your finger-
tips, the batch of berries that you picked,
jam them in a jar, baptize with spit.)

❖ ✦ ❖

Right behind their fuzzy low faces who's that
pushing through the bushes?

                    (a scarecrow)

                                        shapes
like men of crusted snow, numbers slipping
from the night's blackboard

                    (a rash of stars
marching up Gooseberry Hill)

                    the Polack kids

(the nine, nameless, faceless, lined up)

snarling charge.
                    Your lunchbox clattering,
they corner you, pinned to the schoolyard wall.
Terror, lean, a genius, croons, the world
one giant wintry glare.

                    Give them your apple,
sandwiches, the cake.

                    Still they come.

There's more to you than that:
stumbling up the hill, throw them your gloves,
your hat, your coat . . .

                    get him,
            fat little four-eyes,
            teacher's pet,
            momma's tit,
            poppa's snot,

‹ 63 ›

one cent the lot,
                    get him!

                    ✧ ✦ ✧

A shot rings out; the wood a sortie of dark,
trees loop over

                    hunch down and hug

                                        (we all know
what you two are doing in the dark . . .)

faces, passion-twisted, flicker down the street.
Behind them, sprawled like crackling bugs
fallen from the corner lamp, the millhands
on their porches grunt.
                    Belching fumes,
dumped over their lumpy wives, they roar along
the chutes; through the molten heart of the mill
faces heap

            which way did the little bastard go?
Get him, get him!

                    Figures, hurtling, ricochet,
cries of fire,
            Father,

                    where are you?

engines stutter, crushing iron cars,
the sputtering shells crashed over us,
light on light is breaking through . . .

◇ ✦ ◇

(just one step more we reach the top.
Hey, soldier, look. Behind that tree,
that scarecrow's come alive.
      He's scooting
up the hill. After him!)

     Guns glint,
the world slashing like sun on water,
faces flaring, plunging.

      (Watch out,
he's turning. Shoot, shoot I tell you
while you can.
    Atta boy, you winged
him good. He's falling.
      Wait for me!)

His black eyes shadowing, his arms outstretched,
he's clawing through the air, into the dirt,
the rutted sweat, the blood, words spluttering,
caught by that endless moment, face to face,
horror in such white hands,
      and Mother,
Mother slumped into your arms!

July clogged, hunching over you,
a glitter as of snows mixed in with summer;

far below, the same light striking fire
from the waves, the black-shawled, wintry shapes,
bent at the town's one well, beat their clothes.

◇ ✦ ◇

Snow blinkless in his eyes

(the glaring rigid
through your eyes)

the lightning on the stock,
the morning, focused wholly on you, lock:
the vast unblinking icy look,

watch out
for the gun!

the lightning on . . .
can't see,
I'll smash it,
(don't use your gun for that!
All spies got to be taken prisoner.)

No time, supplies,
the cake,
the hat,
the lies.

Strike it, crush that glaring eye forever:
the blow,
again
and again
and again . . .

how many men you trying to kill?

❖ ✦ ❖

A shot
rings out, a sortie of dark,

(hunch down and hug . . .)

crashing iron cars, sputtering shells,
a thousand clashing knives, burst round,

my leg!

       into the dirt, the groans, the rattled
gaspings as you writhe.
                  Frank, Frank!

For Christ sake, got to get you out of here.
Throw your arms round my neck,

                            not so tight . . .
down through roots and rocks,
                        a hornet's seething
mill,
      a beak.
               It stares ecstatic
over you.
              Oh the black lake's stuck.
Across the gunset heavens, redbreast day,
flushed and dripping, feeds a pulpy weed

    the roses by us, sweet and . . .)

⋄ ✦ ⋄

                       choking smell.
A body lurches, cold, stiff, flight fettered
in the air as though a pulse throbbed there;
from some far mountain spring, a common source,
the drops, coursed through your eyes, mouth, breath,
collect.
      How cross this great divide?

                              It's only
the narrow crack where day and darkness meet.
Grab the bird and stamp;
                    and as the earth
begins to rattle,
              jump . . .

                        cavernous waves,
the heave and tumbling sea . . .

                          here's the boat
I promised you . . .

                  east, west, the ship
is tossing; billows clamber summits over you.
The ship is hoisting

                  skull and bones!

                              And those
that smiled—

              butcher, baker, teacher, preacher
undertaker—

              swarthy faces, snarling
at the rail. There's nothing you can trust . . .

that bird, its gold leaf lighting up the way . . .

                    ❖ ✦ ❖

You zigzag like a furled-out, wind-flopt moth.
The breakers, toppled, hurl you onto roaring
rocks.

                    ‹ 68 ›

The stooping, ice-capt mountain shatters;
upright from its evil-smelling cleft
figures flit like smoke shot from your breath
straining for blood to cross the fuming gap.

Darkness belches round,
                    a wild-eyed scream,

how dare you come below?

                    The nine, shapeless,
nameless, mist of dreams clawing, charge,

no, no, you must not drink, not you, not you,
your face, twisted, shifting with every look,
don't make me see it!

                    Having chosen this,
you have no other choice,

                    each wiping out
the last about to speak . . .

✦ ❖ ✦

                    Frank, Frank!
how have you, a wound for mouth, sped here?

Not by what the flesh can do; your breath
North Wind enough, swifter than your black ship,
I, timely as the rites of spring, arrive.

Through these many months and through
the body's dead-of-winter?

> *Through body's cold*
and dead you build your winter.

                              Lament is nearing;
swollen cataract, weeping wails . . .

                    ❖ ✦ ❖

                              your name!
The waters, surging, mouth you.
                         Flesh gives,
white-capt voices,
                the Shrouded Ones.
                              Something sucks

(forgetting boasts them all!)

                    each act, each thought.

Expect to keep that churning pulse, the dark's
and time's, their rancorous secrets, hid forever?
You its one supply of breath, an instant crop:
woman gabble, dreams orgy-fleshed, the dead,
recent and old, fierce by their former fairness.

                    ❖ ✦ ❖

Mother, why do you, pale as hoarfrost glimmer-
ing on leaves, my blood upon your lips,
appear?

        Well you may ask. Not even here
can I embrace you. Your blood you call it.
Your father's blood! Even before your birth

‹ 70 ›

its stranger heart, wrenching itself from me,
sped off with him. Else you would hear
my cry in every drop.
      Yet rightly your question
belongs to me. The pain I knew above
sufficed. I ended it. I am here now because
I wished—no less than have—to be.

          Help me,
Mother.

    Those outstretched hands cannot be meant
for me. Dead I am and, as you are,
dead to you. Much better so than waking
old torment.
     But why pant after two deaths?
The dark haunts you as it haunted me.
My hunger, like these tears, real
in a shadow's eyes, groping, goes on.
And shall until you feed it in yourself.

Why do you who would never let me go—
talk to this fever, Mother,

       but now
no mistake of shielding can be made—
by your own blood, first drunk of me,
I tell you—against the trials you have
to go through still,

     tell this aching
a story as you used to, make it let me
go—why do you avoid me now?

       Try hard
as you will you cannot touch me, any more

than you could, even in that final moment,
call me back.
     Farewell, farewell.
Much as mist can wish, I, once your mother,
wish you, still my son.
       When, the last time,
I hold forth my hand again, you will
indeed be much embraced and, so gathered,
ever stay in me.

     ❖ ✦ ❖

     Oh stay.
       But who
are these following you?

       A mow of women,
faces flashing, most naked of their names
as of their flesh. Not only those you know
but glamors of time your mind cohabits with,
imagination's grossness. Mainly those
who, trusting, gave themselves to you.

And do: as flakes they come, your breath
the blast that whirls them round
as once it failed them in its falterings.
Now through your will working their own, fierce
by their former fairness.
      Last and fairest,

Laura, driving them!
     O why do you,
like a new moon blazing through these clouds
it chars, lour at me?

‹ 72 ›

Never can I forget
That moment's forgetting; see, it boasts
them all! This time you shall not leave

How bear that thrashing in my hands?

✧ ✦ ✧

Even as we lay there, summer's aim,
the roses and the lambs become an ambush,
tenderness, the very moment that
it rose in me, drove terror near, a cold
ferocity, nimbler than the morning,
climbing your eyes . . .

      don't go; don't forgive,
and so forget, me.
     Wind slipt through my fingers,
smoke in the gust of her own sighs,
         she's gone.

But the others do not disdain to drink of me!

Who are you would batter your way down here,
and with your body on? No breaking bloody
bones, no tears of yours, can tide you through.

✧ ✦ ✧

Faces flurry—fevers, buffets—against me.
You pale kingdoms glimmer as from a vault,
like cinders struck: my ancestors, all jostling,
peer.

Not forgotten! The hacked and crushed,
as ashes recognizable, yet voices fleshed,
their gaze, their gestures fixed in speaking only.

Through the mist calls flicker:
                              my youngest dead,
the few I began with, many days feted,
stuffed like hay-fat oxen, then struck down
by a single blow as one butchers at stall
for a wedding banquet;
                              through the gashes fumes:
rotting breath of festered years, youth wasted . . .

                    ◇ ◆ ◇

aether through the suffocating flowers,
high in this narrow room, banked on a cliff
of lilies, a waxen body lies;
                              the tangled
keening, birds beaked in my ears; the dead
weight aching in my hands,

                    birds, trillions of them,
and a giant one,

            the sun,

                    through rushing trees

breaks loose

            and so do I,

                    headlong as always.
Frank, wait for me.

You're the one won't wait.

Round and round you, chortling, leap. The moment
a scampering, rowdy hill, the sunlight sweeps
the boulders on both sides of us like beams
in its abounding will.
     But time won't wait,
the slender body thrashing in my hands,

that and the sly elated betrayals, sweet pain—

worlds and years between, what can I do?

of helplessness . . .

    sinewy moaning winds,
salt-mouthed as the sea, O do not snatch at me.

      ✦ ✦ ✦

Striding like anger, a shooting star, Father!
why do you refuse to look at me?
You're not dead.

    No more, no less than he
has always been to you, scared of a truth
he might have taught.

     The openness: light
explodes. Help me!

    Worlds and years and fears
between, what can he do?

     He rams right through me.

‹ 75 ›

Father, why don't you hear?

                         Get out your hacker,
whack the old bastard, cut down the beanstalk,
the golden pecker,
                    into the mouth and eyes,
that cry,

        the body struggling, warm

                                 (fumes

as from a slaughtered calf)

                    face gone out—
still it stares—that eye, that midnight-black
unblinking eye,
            O all of them and all
these faces, clustered, jutting out, jeer
at me.
        Break them, smash,
                      the lightning locks,
the world clots on the butt . . .

                    ✧ ✦ ✧

But the trajectory of that blow—how easy.
Fellow soldier, since you dare by act
and suffering to come this far, hear one
who knows and so can speak for all the dead.

Gone down into the harrowed, ice-gouged soil,
clods clutched in the ruts, the hammered looks
and screams, smeared on their mouths, in time crop
forth, grape- and lilac-fleshed.

Back now
with a naked truth the living are—even
with this hand clenching the sodden dog tag
round this neck—too sight-lashed for,

> *like you,*

the keeper.

I?

◇ ✦ ◇

The blow, beating the face
together again and
as I watch, a glitter
coils up, hissing, licking at my foot,

like something out of earth and out of snow,
you the keeper: father, mother, children
and their heirs—ghosts you must bear into life.

Oozings from my fingertips, all make,
heart's hammering,
the facets of one eye—
Father, Mother, Frank, the Shrouded Ones,
and . . .
you, the one I killed, barely covered,
green still in the earth, storming through
the others!

Only by this many come:
through your efforts to avoid me, home.
Shun as you will the violence in each thing,
most violently in hand and bird's bright-morning
song, do you think hiding long preserves?

No treasure for us past what we have buried:
passions, loves rejected, banking up
their light and fire in the earth like restless
gems, the bird, the gutted morning, mouths.

Lie stony as you will, relentless time—
its stars more wily than the dark's snowflakes,
their fire needing to be fed—still whirls
and, unabated, will inside the flesh:
pain seeks you; doubt and anguish yearn.

O do not stare at me with such desire.
Shall the wronged, wrong itself, know love?
Please take this, drink with the rest and bless me
with forgetting. Let me go. Through the earth,
and into me, have you not probed enough?

It breaks me

    like the gun-struck thing I am.
Admire sores, black gaping gums, these sockets
filled with nothing.

    No, no! do not stoop
in this fanged light

      ✦ ✦ ✦

    a wedding
banquet . . .
   picnic . . .
     fumy with manure . . .
it's roses, love
  (it's Love, LOVE, L O V E)

‹ 78 ›

that frizzled grin, your eyes like owls, raking,
thrust a shiny darkness through me

                              out
to a clearing—
                    you, Father, Mother, blending,
bob, carcasses sizzling on one spit!

(Love makes the world go round)

                                    It's bending over,
goading them . . . I don't want to see it!
Don't they know I'm here?

                                    Love realizes
nothing but itself, cares for nothing
but itself.

                    The mouth, the wound, the beast
all tooth!

✧ ✦ ✧

                    Who, hissing like wild fowl, a storm
of sickles bristling through my side, are you?

Tribes of tens-of-thousands your blood recalls.

Fie, ravage, crime, decay reek from your mouths.

Your frauds' familiars, those you sped by,
those who claim the life you've long denied.
Try to escape? So ingrained are we in your glance,
its far end clotted with our hair, looking
away draws us nearer.

Out of your breath,
crushed voices, trampled scenes, journeys waiting,
generations grating in one seed,
we burgeon now our summer's withheld might.

Where the end of terror? Fleeing the furies

hauls them into sight.

The beast at me,
the tooth!

✧ ✦ ✧

Through the length of your whole being
know it, feel it; then go, look after my life
and yours. That snaky head, a kindred too,
you must not yet confront. Nor swaddle in,
sipping the maggot's milk, homespun of spider.

Some things—the crag, the granite sea, the slug,
this mouth that grinds incessantly in you—
cannot be turned into the human. All
that we can do is try, while we are men,
to meet them humanly.
That time will come
when it must come, the time that does not seek
us out by name and does not recognize,
forgive or smile.
Now I, having served,
return to earth that bore me of which I am—
in all these years of wandering and dread—
return. You too return, to these I leave,
the living isle, the human hour.

Where men
in cunning pass the wily fox, in skill
of greed exceed the swine, dawn also dwells;
still dawn tracks out her dancing-floor.
The night involved, the Hunter on his knees,
see the great flock nestling in that song.

Remember me and these, but locally,
like lilac, iris, thickly clustered grapes,
and in conspirings of wind and sea.

❖ ✦ ❖

Remember you? Nothing can be forgotten.
To be a living vault, inheritor
of all your griefs, spring brings flowers to
and summer chokes with plenty; to feel them
thrusting over me, the roses, puffy
with my breath.
         Yet woods in every leaf
look away; even as I touch, in pools
blue-lipt water chars.
         How can I push
this body to the top of my corruption-
crammed and -trammeled journey?

❖ ✦ ❖

         The hillside,
rubbled cries, is tumbling down. A green
man, giant as he rises,
         something monstrous
out of snow,

                    stalks reach out, July
bristling bayonets in shocks, a bellied
commerce, everywhere suckling a dead man's bones.

My name

                    I never heard!

                              multitudinous
in skittering leaves an autumn long, cicadas,
twisted sounds, in hail of skillful winds,
handling your black ship's shrouds.
By such gear morning comes.
                              Back now

as the earth once pivoted in your wrist

into the motion, complex music
of the Pleiades, one with Orion,
rounding up his game he once pursued
and fled, like bees herded into dawn.

                    ✧ ✦ ✧

The ship pitches, giving up one last
concerted cry,

                    no less than men and beasts,
sky and the creature sea ride in its hold
as in that cry,

                    slows to his bed.
                              Slobber
in every breath, through the hissing aether,
bit by bit, finger joined to finger,

the bird is gathering me.
                              I twirl in its beak,
a seed, a twig, burst at once into a wood,
the dawn perched askingly among its limbs.

Through the mist and through the hard scrutinous
light, thick flakes whirling, faces shape
again.

       Soon, the window thawed, its frost
like mountain flowers strewn upon these day-
heaped sheets, the world, barefoot in my eyes,
as walking to and from my bed, once more
begins.

FROM

The Medium

«1965»

The Medium

Fog puffed from crusted snow, rain sputters
midnight over them. Her words, a kind
of browsing in themselves, rise, cloud-bound,
by him in the bed.
              She says, "I know
now why I have no memory. It's come to me,
a revelation. I must keep my thinking
open; I am not, like others, scribbled
all over by whatever happens."
                    He answers,
"Revelation? That's what you've always been
to me; by way of you have I not slithered
under the skin of things?"
                 "Cleansed of words,
my fears and doubts cast off, the fears
that words invent, I see each thing, free
at last to its own nature, see it free
to say exactly what it is."
              "As for our primo-
genitor," he chimes in, "beside his twi-
lit doorway, bent after the long day's chores
on the seraphic visit, meantime calling
things by their first name again."
               "You won't
believe that people waken in my sleep
and like the moon, self-enlightened, speak
a language I don't know, move in a language
so itself one needn't know."

                              "Dreams,"
he nods, "do such things, like you attune
the dim as well as the emphatic phrases
I live in, the world become a bob-
bingly translucent globe, that round,
piped like Aeolus' impassioned winds
into a tiny bag,
                    then popped, grape-
sweet, upon my tongue, for you beside me
sounding its fanfare. Such cornucopia
your lip and hand."
                      "How you do go on!
Unless you curb these peacock speeches you
love strutting in, how will you ever hear
another's words?
                    Now listen to me. My father
lives again, in the special space I keep
for him here in my sleep, as he really is,
nothing but his fundamental voice,
directness daylight always must obscure,
cluttered as we are with long dead habits
and with failures, rage, my own and his,
encrusting us."
                  The dream flushed on her still
addresses him through her without a sound:
"The time will come when your time comes;
the role meant for you slamming shut,
none of your wit, your artful dodgings,
able to hide you then, each thing you do
 at last will prove effective, like a lion
grinding through your side."
                              As moonlight
brims the fog, he hears, in books lined up
around them, richly scored, a honey pouring
through the words, the language passing
speakers, too imperious for words.

Clothes Maketh the Man

(to be read aloud awkwardly)

How hard it is, we say,
how very hard. Clearly no one can say
these cluttered lines and make them
stride or make them stay. No actress
in the land—the best have tried—
can find a pattern or a rhythm
in our day's befuddled monologue.

Concede, I say, a role to test the mettle
of a Bernhardt, who, wigged, without a leg
and in a ragged voice could—so they say—
strike any rock-like audience to tears,
this with only the alphabet.
      Maybe,
you say, maybe. But then the alphabet
by Racine, no less.
    And I am depressed.
Ah me, I am depressed to think how we,
with many more outspoken words, submit
to mumblings, silence, only answer
fitting our despair.
     How hard it is,
we say, how very hard, to find ourselves
stuck in such muck.
     Oh well, I say,
maybe when we haven't understood
each other long enough, that muck will
harden into a stuff that we can carve.

Already Goya knew the sharp rebuff
of nakedness. With nothing between
he almost wrung his naked Maja's neck,

‹ 89 ›

as though he'd stuck the head of one girl,
a much beloved, on the body of another
(for less aesthetic uses, say), and they
would not set, not in the daring solvent
of his paints.
          His Maja draped was
a far different matter. I say, I never
thought I'd prefer a dressed girl to one
undressed. Even for me, I see, it's later
than I guessed.
             So let's go home to bed,
Renée, and dress and dress and dress.

A World to Do

"I busy too," the little boy
said, lost in his book
about a little boy, lost
in his book, with nothing

but a purple crayon
and his wits to get him out.
"Nobody can sit with me,
I have no room.
            I busy
too. So don't do any noise.
We don't want any noise
right now."
         He leafs
through once, leafs twice;
the pictures, mixed with windy
sighs, grow dizzy,

world
as difficult, high-drifting
as the two-day snow that can
not stop.
How will the bushes,
sinking deeper and deeper,
trees and birds, wrapt
up, ever creep
out again?
Any minute now the blizzard,
scared and wild, the animals
lost in it—O the fur,

the red-eyed claws, crying
for their home—may burst
into the room. Try words
he's almost learned
on them?
He sighs, "I need a man here;
I can't do all this work
alone."
And still, as though
intent on reading its own
argument, winter continues
thumbing through itself.

In the Round

Catching yourself, hands lathery
and face ajar, inside the glass,
you wryly smile; watching, you know
you're in for it:

                    and in the twinkle
of your eye the horny butting goat
and jutting horny bull, the weasel,
goose bedraggled, and the wren
with greedy bill go flashing by;
there too, recoiled as from the shadow
of itself in a teetering pool, claws
contracted to one cry, the spider
crouches in its den.
                    What gusto
can it be that blows its violence
through a locust's violin, mad summer
burnishing in such midge mouths?

These the routine heroes, poised,
in resolution black as bulls,
deadlocked like a din of warriors
grappling centaurs—prizes near:
a heifer nibbling grass; the rouged
and gossamer girl, nothing diaphanous
as the fearful hope that flits,
a fire's touch, inside her breath,
each prize forgotten—on a vase.

One wonders how the clay withstands
not only time, but what its hands,
great hearts, command from one another,
art and earth, the audience amazed.

Still, though clay crack, necks
break, twitchy as a cock, they stand,
engrossed and going on, a Bach
of a beetle, strutting like a yokel,
nightlong at its tongs and bones.

Studying French

some thirty years too late
(the rhythms do declare themselves,
the glints, through clumsy clouds,
through stiff-as-frozen clods,
the flowers in their revery),

I, who love our English words
and loll in them against
the several terror and the cold
like any little furry animal
grown cocky in his hole, begin

to understand past supple words
the language you and I grope
toward and, reaching, wander in
among the periods of doubt,
those long, benumbing nights

when ice caps seem to travel
us at their own stately speed
and fury like a moony beast,
a speechless, glacier-capable,
goes poking its rough tongue,

so searching, into the crevices,
the weaknesses, of everything.
For one long given over
to another tongue this French
is much too hard. It makes me

doubt myself, my easy hold
on everything, and everything.
I who debonairly strolled

(I rallied them, I twitted them
with double-talk) among my words

like one among his animals,
once wild, but now their strength,
their rippling colors, blazoned
on him, can smell once more
the threatening smolder, smoke

behind them, open fields so fine
for pouncings and hot blood,
the void in flower we go out
to meet, hand clutched in hand,
as it ransacks us for its tutoyer.

Into Summer

Some days ago, to stop the leaping
weeds, on both sides of the path
workmen scorched these fields.
A short time after, as he passed
the charcoal-velvety, zigzag tracks,
he smelt the strange blend of the
burnt and the growing.
                        But now,
just over the black, something flags,
green flicked here and there,
but mostly a transparent papery
brown, like stubborn ghosts caught
in the fire and yet come through,
nodding as though to say, "This is
as much as we can do."

And he who
tried to pierce the classroom tedium,
to move his students to a grove,
a clearing where the green remains,
recalls some struggled into words,
then fallen back, eyes flickering
a second as though caught with sun.

And they, like one's best hopes
and feelings, singed yet wrangling
through, knowing nothing but the need
to go on, into summer?
                              Soon,
of their own greed and by the tangle
of numbers, the weeds will do
what the greasy fire was meant to.

But now each must heed the music
mumbling in him—in some crazy way,
on top of the brown, green sticks out,
and a whitish, tiny kind of flower—
that strange blend of the burnt
and the growing.

On Stuffing a Goose
(after overhearing some students talk knowingly of D. H. Lawrence)

Is this fame then and what it is to be
really alive, to go on living after flesh,
having failed, has been officially
hauled away?
                  To cast a moment's spell

upon some distant man and girl, a feeling
of familiarity in a gust of fragrance
in a summer's night,
                    of loneliness
made roomier as they recall his anguish,
as though flesh alone, one time and place,
one wife, a single set
                    of friends
were too confining and that life must be
let out to mine its basic cadence finally
in our pondering of it,
                    free of any
obligation save the pleasure that we take
in it. . . . My father was a great hand
at stuffing geese.
                    In the cellar dark
he'd keep one penned. Knees grappling it,
he'd ram a special mash with dippers
of water down its throat.
                    In time
that crate began to bulge; past waddling,
goose managed only belchy squawks.
We knew it ready.
                    Somewhere in all this
I have a sense of what it is to be really
alive. Somewhere in the celebration
of that goose,
                    throned on a shiny
platter, for its mellow crackling skin
a jovial martyr, piping savors of a life
fulfilled,
                    our heart's gladness
in the occasion of picking the juicy meat
from the sides and the bones, in that
and remembering the sense abides.

FROM

The Last Day and the First
«1968»

The Last Day and the First

The stocky woman at the door,
with her young daughter "Linda" looking
down, as she pulls out several copies
of *The Watchtower* from her canvas bag,
in a heavy German accent asks me:
"Have you ever thought that these
may be the last days of the world?"

And to my nodding "Yes, I have,"
she and the delicate, blonde girl
without a further word, turning tail,
sheepishly walk away.
                    And I feel
for them, as for us all, this world
in what may be its last days.
And yet this day itself is full
of unbelief, that or marvelously
convincing ignorance.
                    Its young light
O so tentative, those first steps
as of a beginning dance (snowdrops
have already started up, and crocuses
we heard about last night the teller's
children quickly trampled in play)

make it hard not to believe that we are
teetering on creation's brink all over
again. And I almost thrill with fear

to think of what will soon be asked
of us, of you and me;
                         am I at least
not a little old now (like the world)
to be trembling on the edge
of nakedness, a love, as Stendhal
knew it, "as people love for the first
time at nineteen and in Italy"?

Ah well, until I have to crawl
on hands and knees and then can crawl
no more, so may it every Italian-
returning season be, ever the last
day of this world about to burst
and ever for blossoming the first.

Caliban Remembers

I

                          Might
have gone with them. Might. To be—
I heard their scheming—a strange fish,
seasick on land, lurching in shadows,
a monster they, tormenting, make.
No one for me. Not my master's kind
with perfumes stinking, auks at courting.
Nor to me true friends those two
I fell in with.
                Oh fell in with,

a horse-pond for our pains, and over
ears, scum sticking to, thick scum.

"Putrid fish," all jeered at me.
As if, from king on down, they did
not take their fishy turn in the sea.
As in the way they reached this shore.

On such a day—moons marching by
my marking time—sat I out here,
sat, shading me, beneath this cliff.
The sea, one blinding wave, bulged round.
The sun had soaked deep into it,
into each bush, each tree. Had soaked
into these rocks until they shook
with light.
        There—I fished then too—
a great wind suddenly blowing up,
foam in its mouth, a bloody shriek,
that boat.
        Again and again surf broke
on it. Yet sparkling everywhere,
a blaze that, sizzling, blazed the more,
boat, gliding over this cove's jag rocks,
rode in.
        By then, for lightning's rifts,
one wave hot after me the sea,
I scuttled off, got me to
my cave's dark cleft and, glad at last
to have it, hid.
        My rod dangles,
once more sways the waters, swelling
from the line. New shadows risen,
noises I hear past what such brooding
high-noon brings. Hummings out of the sea

and the air, out of the woods?

Long tides

ago, I remember, hardly remember,
there were others. Low voices, rough,
could find me out, prod me, please.
No wasp's bite sharper, whirring through,
no grape-burst sweeter. Vague at best
now, like that name he'd knot to me.

Yet things I have belonged to them.
This gown, a giant ringdove's rainbow-
downy hood, I lounge in, tatters
and all, once my master at his magic
needs must wear, with his rod fishing
outlandish cries, their creatures in them,
from air and sea.

Lurked among books

he left. At times, efts in heaped leaves
as out of sleep, they pop. Yet as I
bend they fade, day after day
farther away.

But next to my hand

this pebble, blinked at me, a trinket
it might have been, dropped that time
I stumbled on her dreaming here,
dazzled by her still, as her glass,
cast off, raised to the face, a look
flashing, says she's, passing, teasing,
by behind me.

Chalk-faced, hair

sleeked down, no otter better, stalked
behind her, basking in her light,
so darking me who saw her first,
that Ferdinand.

How push back

this crinkle badgers brow?

Witch she,

‹ 102 ›

not my poor mother, I tweaked as ever,
as a jay its secretest feather.
And most, blood at the heart hopping,
dare I speak out her name.
                              Sometimes
taste still—remembering bubbles—gust
of that liquor. Cloud-casked surely,
music fermented. Those two bidding me
drink, one gulp, and no more goading
for me. God I, the sky my gliding,
earth, everything in it my subject,
far below.
                    Now, if ever they were,
gone. Even my sleep, only rarely
whispering in it, slips free of them.

From the thicket, peeping, watched
the long ship I helped stow fruit, fish,
water aboard sweep out and silently,
its sails confused with clouds, folding,
unfolding, melt as though the wind,
seeing them go, blew merrily.

At first I also, kicking up heels,
scattered round their garments, linens,
books. At first. But after—how find
again that whole belonging mine
before they came?—and worst those days
when I, a smoke, fume through my hands,
loneliness whelms me.
                              Had I only
his book's good company, that company
it kept waiting, perfect, on him,
humble the world, I'd lord it truly.

My rod, sprouting though it did
from the staff he thought forever buried

and I plucked it, swish as it will
to rouse the breezes, rustle the sea,
fares forth no revelries like his,
nor no revelations neither.

Times I'd welcome the old, heavy
chores, his orders at roughest irk,
echoed in cramps, nips, pinches,
hedgehogs packed and inchmeal wedging
through me.
    Times they rack me still,
those pokes, side-stitches (feared at first—
my shivers mounted—he'd returned;
aches he had, all kinds, fit
for each part of the body, aches
he must have stuffed in hollow branches
sealed with pitch, then like the noises
from his pipe, at will puffed out);
and shapes they do inside the dark,
torching me that I slubber in bogs,
on mad bushes burr me, furzes clawing.
But now not meant for me, no ape-
mouthing sprites behind them to mock,
not anger, only themselves.
      Themselves
those plumes awag at the water's edge,
draggled through mire, flood, yet dry,
a play straight out of the spume?
      Not those
from the ship again, untouched, a miracle,
unless the shine they sport be sea's
(my master bragged he kept them so),
but tailing one another, great bugs.

Well, whatever comes pleases me,
my state on the isle. Its flocks and herds,

its slyest creatures, these, as I pluck
for hides, food, feathers, tribute
also in their squawky cowering,
scrape to me King. Tame too
as they never were for those. Long days
I loll, ruler and subjects the same.

Even so things I learned, some,
nag at me still, names that, shimmering,
as I would clamp jaws to, dissolve.
And the faces glimmered out at me
from bush and sky, tide-riding shapes.

Came on her in this very cove,
swimming still on her, whiter, rounder
than a wave, open to the sun.
Then I understood his daily command:
"Stand upright, stand!" Upright I was,
knew at last what he meant by "Be
a man." Saw she was gone there, torn
out by the roots. Wish in sudden,
flushed kindness, pity, give her mine,
all.
    But tiptoed, manhood in hand,
to surprise her, completed while she slept,
as by magic—was it our fires,
crossing, drew him?—scepter quivering,
upright, he appears. Eyes blazed
on me, cares, it seems, nothing
I have learned my lesson, quick
to obey.
        Fear he had I'd fish
his pond? Oh no, not fish it, stock it!
Who else was there to do her turn,
so save the day for the likes of me,
and him as well, on the island?

Not all his magic, age, can angle
new foundlings, me more, out of air.
Even now loss wrings me.
                    Still his words,
crackling, strike me everywhere stony,
yet shaking too. One frown farther
I had been done.

    II

                    But hear that hiss.
A rumbling scrabble, skin atwitch,
the sea would speak?
                    Lo! the rod
grows taut, throbs, humming, in my hands.

There, dripping, spluttering thick sighs,
bobs a swollen, slippery thing.
Some odd, mad fish I've caught!

Clutch it.
        A book!
                    Alive again:
inside its blotched pages, seasick,
for all the sights, blood-chilling worlds,
it's gulped, words, through fingers slither-
ing minnows, hop.
                    Mixed in its spells now,
nymphs once cropped, nymphs and urchins,
romping, couple, splotched purple swirling.

Clouds my master called this world,
clouds and dreams (a sorcerer then,
a stronger, over him, mouthing things,
wording us, thus puffed into being,
browsing on our aches and rages?).

Such waking cloud this book's become.
Reading before, its gnat-words fidgety,
not hard enough!
                Yet some, tails flouncing
as if plunged into the sea, beswamped
by smudgy ink, I know again.

Put ear to page. Hear something.
Grumbling steady, far off collecting.
His voice, is it, penned in the words?

That voice—like it no other sound—
which, first stroking, then grown gruff,
kept its kindness for this book
he turned to more and more, the rough
of it all that was left and there
to abuse me.
             Master he may have been,
yet could do nothing without me. Not,
unless I, fetching sticks, patched fire,
rouse his magic, its high-flown tricks.
Whatever his flights, had to return
to this island, his cell, me.
Never could, whatever his flights,
go back to his country till they came
with that ship.
              I alone propped him, kept
as earth does sky, else dropped in the sea.

Why then should I not use it also?
Shake me out music, that brave host,
showering praises, presents isle-heaped:
luscious fruits flung from the trees;
liquors clouds, cask-big, split,
pour down, thirsty for my tongue;
fish pied flying in out of waves

‹ 107 ›

as the sea itself, glistening, bows,
then at my feet stows dutiful ships,
with treasure crammed as palm-tall hives,
their honeycombs oozing.
                              Maybe can,
why not, raise one fair as she,
a dozen, sea-blooms, wreathing her,
bent on one thing only, hooked,
dolphin-sleek, dished in the sun,
one thing: pleasing me.
                              Cloudy as sky,
bow-taut, is growing, better begin.
Drape the robes about me, so.
Wagging the staff, half crouch, half stiff,
nose raised as if snuffling scents,
the music working under things.

Now find the place in the book.
                              Here,
the lines most faded. Head nodding
right, then left, both eyes rolling,
till body drops away.
                              (Never knew
I spied on him mumbo-jumboing,
then jutting ear as if he thought
to hear answer. Was there something,
mutters, say the air's bright crest,
aflutter, speaking, speaking I
now seem to be hearing out of these
drowsy trees?)
                              Oh, could he see
me now, his lessons like his scepter
clutched, the earth, the sea, the cloud-
packed sky about to wake, how pleased
he'd have to be.
                              I can, mouth plumped,

almost repeat that rounded phrase
finished off in a hiss.

                    Lo, now, lo!
Even as I say it, darkness hedges,
crowding out of the sea.

                    Beware!
A lightning crashes, fire's scribble
scratchy down sky; and that oak, sky-high,
falls at my feet.

                One twig closer
and I had been—homage truly!—ever
crowned.

                Wake that squall again?
Watching him manage it, hearing
out of it bellows, no beasts madder,
demons not (suppose more loosed
than he could handle?), shuddered me
through.

                There, high on squall's ruff,
an osprey its spray, a cormorant beaking,
in the distance riding, gay as a porpoise,
the ship bobs that took them off!

Desire that: my master back,
she, the others, firewood, fast rooted
where I dumped it, ache in my bones,
the play—I ever cast for monster,
slave, with real blows in it, hurting
words—to be played over and over?

Oh no. Now that his book's mine,
my lackeys they.

                  Ah the sweet tasks
I would conjure for them as—standing,
upright, rigid, by, they glare,
if cast down, deadly looks—I lie

in my flower-puffed bed, she, flower
among flowers, by me, mistress
to my least worded, far-fetched whim.

And him I bid bring turtle eggs,
struggle through fanged briers for berries,
prickles too of bees he must snatch
choicest honeysacks from.
                       The others,
husked of rapiers, ruffs, fine airs,
down on all fours, the beasts they are,
cuff them, kick. Out of their yelping,
as master's pipe could ply a storm,
pluck music.
                  One bears me a bowl
brims rose water, petals swimming;
and dabbling hands, on another I wipe.
Then order these pour the good wine
down throat. Or "Scratch the regal back
with porcupine." Wanting the palace
his book shows, "Scoop out that fen.
Put rocks over there. There. And there."
And, put, not liking it, "Put back
again."
         But as they, drooping, sigh,
their struts and frets, wildfire plots,
gone out, would I not let them be,
him most, most haggard for these labors
far beyond his years, and he, first,
landing on this shore, enjoying
for a time what he found here, most kind?
As I enjoyed, a time, the silks,
the warmth, the tunes he (she more) soothed
against me.
            Best in that moment when,
as now, shadows deepen the wood.

Then, he piping, I sprawled by,
the notes bubbling, moonlight dewy
on them, as in her eyes, already
gleaming secrets of caves, sea-kept,
she sang. And winds and waves, chins set
in their hands, the stars, leant down, peering
ever harder as darkness ripened,
also sang. One radiant sound,
the earth and sky involved in it,
soaked into me, I shook with light.

So he, sitting over me, listened,
I at fishing not more still.
Points at things, making fish mouths,
stranger noises. And a mote
baiting my eye, a mayfly twirling,
whole day, if tiny, on midnoon,
prods with "Mind, mind!" till at last,
no salmon swifter thrashing waters,
flipped above the spray, the word,
words loosed, stream from my mouth.
Joy in him then, love like my own.
Eager to show me this thing, that.
His books spread out before me, shared,
I learn to pin their swart bugs down.

A book, it seems, for everything,
for things that cannot be and never
could. Had one even showing me
and in it called "Caliban"
because I fed, not less gladly
than on ants, on men. How could I,
no man being here? And think
of eating those, washed up, rotten,
worse than flotsam, on this shore!
To them alone such name belongs

‹ III ›

who would, not cold, not hungry, kill.
(The name I had I never told,
with mother buried who gave it me.)

But best of all that warbling book,
as on a cloud inscribed, about clouds.
The world so graved, growing, changes,
one thing into another, like a cloud,
its women turning, as the pages
do, into a tree, a brook,
a song. Who would have thought their looks,
their voices, now only a windy leaf,
a rivulet, the hearer's tears
start forth, the world seen newly
in their light.
           But am not I,
not merely stone, such changeling too?
So she, in one day sped from childhood
stalk-thin, gawky, into woman.
What I became she could not see
but only heard, as I would sigh,
the same old shaggy husk of me,
as that god, changed, so the book said,
into a bull for love, must bellow.

His books I browsed on. All but one.
No matter how I yearned, heaven
it loomed, mocking, over my head.
And that the book I saw him lost
in, sitting by the fire, listening
to its gossip, mingled with the jiggly
words, his stare outglaring embers.
That tongue, so good at wagging, flogging,
little about him then but as it
jogs off on its own. And the eye
that easily caught me out, no eye
for me, a thing that never was.

Mornings too, quick to me earth,
the berries restless in their plot,
the sky as well, I knew it time
to tend the day. But he shut away
as though, beyond those pages marked,
no light, no joy, can bloom.
                              Damned be
such book when world in lark enough,
in filbert and in plum, cries out
that I become a winged hearing,
lapping tongue, and those the ground-
work eyes and hands abound them in,
my feelings, ripened as they ripe.

Let him be buried in his glimmering
dark while I sprawl in the sun,
in busy, slow pleasure running hot
fingers over me. Or, plunging,
lounge inside the thicket, tickled
by the shade, webs buzzing, leaf-mold
rotting on mold, a wood-bug sometimes
gulped with a berry.
                      Long hours on
and into the night within my fingers,
under my lids, the daylight tingles,
tingle too along my dreams
those sozzled smells, the fruits as when
I munched on them.
                      And he, after,
the fire gone out? Grey, ash-grey.

Yet that one book, even as I have it,
is it better than the world, telling
where winds are woven, snows, sundowns,
showing them being made, and played
out as its owner bids?
                      Some god

must have bestowed it on my master,
else dropped it—as later he did—
lying open, wind-leafed, wind-sighing,
like this earth, and my master found it.

Time and place forgot, he wandered
in it, blissfully bound by soundings
he could make.
          So on this island
all seasons at once or, as he wished,
seasons from strange countries,
mountains in his cell and light
as clouds, tall mountains flaming round
the embers, goddesses too and sprites—
the rites of them.
          But then he saw—
perhaps the days between the spells,
their willingness to work, grew longer,
harder, or he woke, ash-grey—
what empty dream he'd snared him in,
learned the lesson I had always known:
with that book to give himself, to dive
into the thrilling waters, chilled
at times, hard buffeting, this world,
this life is?
          No, angrier he grew,
his words mocking him. Angrier,
words like blows.
          Never knew,
I, finding words he did not know,
like new, hidden nests could show him,
eggs speckled with writing brighter
than his book's, sly birds, the topmost
sky still breathing from their wings,
in their songs still.
          Then he might

have, once more trusting me, entrusted
the isle, as mate his daughter.
                        Instead
that feathery, ribboned thing! May he,
filched my place with the logs, her fancy
also, drown this time for good,
a delicate food lining fish bellies,
sweet between my royal teeth
(Caliban called, Caliban be).
Then, who knows, she might, seeing
him at last so much in me,
me like the more.
                    Or, better, let him,
soaked enough, grown scaly through
and through, yanked out, Caliban me.
If he, pale sprout, could supplant me,
why I not him? Three times as much
as his dragged, staggering, poor armful,
he a king's son, I can haul.

Our names with their three syllables,
two mountains humping a crouched "i"—
Cal-i-ban and Ferd-i-nand,
Ferdinand and Caliban
(somewhere in between Miranda)—
like enough so that the mouth
which shaped out his with loving breath,
a trill the birds would stop to hear,
to mine could be as kissing-kind?
Ah, well, would she ever have—
how could she—loved a thing like me?

Why, instead of all that work,
those lessons, slow, dull, scratchy,
did my master, worlds at hand,
not turn me presto into prince?

Sea, fire, sky he managed
featly; but I too much for him,
an earth magic alone could never change?

Never, as he sought to stuff me
with his learning, asked he me
my thought, my feeling. All I was
was wrong, to change. All he wished
was aping, my face wrought to look,
a mirror, more and more like his.

III

The book in hand, past teaching now.
Try the last words.
                    That grating stink!
Up it dredges from grottos, bogs,
sunk under the sea.
                    And swelling out,
choking the air, one racketing cry.

He's back, overseeing me, making me
do what I do? Or Setebos
with his accursed crew, sneaked in
at last and most to devil me—
who else is left to feed their hate?—
for being driven off?
                    A crack
as though the earth is splitting!
                                    Out there,
lit, the ocean spouts. One monstrous
fish?
      No, upright, like a mighty
man in flashing robes and roars—
would I could give this book to him!—
I see it, see his city, so he

called it, climbing the skies, its spires,
cloud-piled, the gardens multiplied
with gilded fountains, songs torch-lit,
and women, each a little bower,
while far below dark fires rage,
the swamp on which such city's built.

Like torrents crashing over a crag,
aimed, writing its zigzag, a lightning
dashes over me.
                  Now crumbles,
tumbling, drags the outermost rim
of the isle with it!
                     My doing? Have done
no lone thing yet brings me one crumb
of joy; no singing—only this howling,
sky clipt open, trolls my name.

What if, the salt marsh flushed and pounced
on me, I move the moon, the sea
rushed over the isle, I among mollusks
down there, for sharks a crunchy music?

Ass enough that time I dreamed
I could, with those two clumsy sots,
set me free, be king. Master
I called one, god, licking his foot,
and he, for all the sack in him,
not mire good enough to cake
my master's boot. And I believed
he'd bottled moonshine, music, himself,
the moon's own man, dropped with them!

Oh lessoned I am. Off with the gown.
Break the wand. Before this book,
more than ever my master did,

‹ 117 ›

rules over me, ruins entirely,
drown it again. Never wanted it
in the first place.
                    So let it sink.
Dissolved into the restlessly paging
(seems to be reading it), gurgling sea,
the nymphs and dolphins schooled by it,
it may, sea-changed, sigh out its message.
As now.
              Whatever his tempest brought
about, this one washes me clean
of them, blundering on their tottery
two feet (upright they pride themselves
on being!), in broad daylight bethicketed,
wilder than night. And all the time
plotting.
              Then why so foolish
as to toss his power away and, naked,
return to a world bustling with men,
his brother, my silly crew, repeated
a thousand, thousand times over? Expose,
as well as himself, his dear daughter
to infections, plagues, far past the work
of scummy ponds!
                    Devils they said
haunting this island. No least devil
till they arrived. Not all the toads
and frogs this island spawns could quell
the viper in them. Devils he sailed
away with, devils, waiting, hordes,
to dog him all his life's last days.
Think of a world, an island like this,
swarmed with them, their schemings, brawls!

Winds blow over me, the crooning
night air, free now, full of nothing

< 118 >

but its own breath, serenades
the locusts chirr, scents of the sea
and this my island, twining with
what stars are pouring.
                              Yet, not burrs
snarled tighter in the hair, they cling,
that manyed voice, as in a sea-
shell, ebbing, wailing, far inside
into my ear.
                       Fingers remember
the bowl they brought, his hand on it,
hers, the water gushed forth, sparkling,
laughter, worlds. I polishing,
how it gleamed out pleasure, over-
wrought with my face, fitting in
beside hers, his.
                          Its carvings music
swelling to the eye, the finger,
from the pipe the piper on it
raises who is blowing out
the rounded, cloud-big, smoky sky,
I enter it, the little landscape
centered in thick trees a wind
in fragrant waves is wreathing, wreathing
me, shapes watching.
                              Him I see,
see her approaching. Eyes smart,
fingers tingle, taught sly snaggings
of silk, as eyes are caught by her
skirt rustling, the drop of her lids
a deafening tide in the blood till I,
battered as by that liquor's gust,
for the flooding over me drown.

Oh no, not that again, not me
gone in the dark of too much light.

Not bowls, nor touching words, to push
me out of me.
              There, smash bowl
to the earth, the dust it after all
is. And through its shattered pieces,
him and her, those others scattered,
I tramp free, free as the air.

Not lost, all ebbed away as water,
precious wines words keep as casks,
for that he would have taught?
                    Too high,
he rose, reached past earth, while I
slumped, an earth, below.
              At last
as he gave up me, gave up spells,
mind changed, chose man, the life
that all men lead, a magic, dream
more than enough?
             Preferred the bowl
as much at breaking, robes faded
and faces, dyings, their plots too,
their hates.
            And most that momentary,
everlasting human touch—to touch
Miranda's hand again! A queen now,
joy of children throning her
as they, shrill, ruckle round her knees?
And he, does he live still, sometimes,
head shaking, bent in some forgotten
corner over an old book,
muttering maybe "Caliban"?—
the fearful, wide-open risk of it,
touch that runs like lightning through,
feeling, as men feel, as men call it
real.

No matter how I squat,
leaves thick and dark mixing, dark
from inside owl wings, bat's screechy
darting, my cave sealed off, I stick out,
prickly, listening.
             How I long
to hear once more those me-completing
voices. Come back, would cast me
at their feet. And yet . . . alone, alone
as he must be, loathing, pitying, loving.

A Letter from the Pygmies

Dear Whoever-You-Are-That-You-Are,

Whatever chance this has of reaching You,
I write to bring You up to date.

I cannot, little as I join them
in their skills at hunting,
undertake Your tigers. Rarely
do Your lofty auks invite me
to the confabs of their aeries.
Pastimes Leviathan delights in
never has he offered to share
with me; never has he proffered
island back or cove-snug belly.

Still there is the cat Hoppy
who, whatever our blandishments,
as he cannot drop his creaturehood,
claws flying his pleasure, takes me

‹ 121 ›

some good distance into Your creation;
dew starlit on his fur, the fields
wherein Your wonders grow he smells of.
And when, unblinkingly, he fixes me
as though he were upon the scent

of rabbit, mouse, or other friend,
I know the instantaneous delight
of terror. So elation finds me
in the chickadee that bobs
upon our thrashing window-bush,
skullcap awry like any plucky Jew's,
a Job in synagogue of ashes, cries;
as Hoppy bats the pane, it never
budges from our fat-packed rind.

In short, though there's a scheme
afoot to blow Your ark and all in it
to smithereens, to pitch a cloudy,
climbing tower will convert the earth
into one tomb, I know by feelings
craning, preening, deep inside
the ark's still riding, riding high.

So from time to time, what time remains,
I'll do my best to keep in touch with You.

Faithfully Yours,
Theodore

The Life of . . .

for Bill and Dorothy

I

"So there we were stuck
in Alassio all that rotten winter
in a rented house, no one around
but puffed-up Germans, and nothing
to read beyond a pair I can't abide,
Boswell and Johnson, the latter worse
than his crony.
                 And nothing to do
but struggle on through that wretched
Life of . . . . How I loathed it!"

II

"Ah, my friend," I say, "that's what,
more or less, it always comes to,
one book to a customer.

Storms clattering through their lines,
some, if they've the time for it,
wonder how they'll ever learn to follow,
let alone unravel, their chaotic plot.

Others, it's true, are luckier:
richer text, with pictures, colored,
every second page and gilt-edged, bound
in buckram that's the latest rage.

But each of us, like it or not,
is stuck in his own Alassio, waiting
there, flopped open."

‹ 123 ›

III

"Actually,"
my friend's wife now breaks in, "after
the first two summer months, after
the Germans left, the flashy decorations
nailed up on the shops for them
pulled down,
          and the Italians
gradually appearing, rotten winter
and all, we grew to love the town,
admit it.
        Why, whatever the weather's
ludicrous fits, just our garden alone,
with its crazy, tangled, nonstop blooming—
    roses, geraniums, and the rest—
through shattered bottles, cans, and every
kind of litter.
         Or those narrow, dark,
malarial streets at the end of which,
on our long walks, the sea greeted us
like a blaze burst through a tunnel.

And that's not all. Have you forgotten
the forlorn little fishing-fleet going out
each night as we went to bed and, at dawn,
returning as we woke,
            threw open
the shutters, and watched behind it
a red heaped up on the creamy water,
the sun rising, as though, towed
in, part of the catch?
        And a bit later
too, once we learned our way around,
the mountain that we loved to climb,
looming over the town and high enough

with its paths twisting to the top
so that one seemed to see—
                                             a new day
previewed there, just as it was forging
forth—eye to eye with the moon."

Far Out, Far In

I

What we go out for
we often do not know,
though some are lucky
thinking that they do,

like those priests
in their white cassocks
diving into the canals
of Venice after the cross,

or those explorers
plunged, perverse enough,
through swamps and jungles,
most at home when lost,

and those luckiest
of all perhaps, gone out
simply for the pleasure—
limbs set, mind—of going,

as from this beach
a stand of grown pines

closes in, protected past
that by a mountain range.

II

On stilt-like poles
nets, dangling, shimmer
in the wind coral-crimson,
minnow-golden, seaweed-

green—in the fish
one wishes to lure one
must anticipate varieties
of taste; nearby glass

knobs for floaters
that craze the sunlight;
also mats adazzle with
fish laid out to dry;

and boats in whose
high-pooped shade men,
women and children sort
the day's many-sided catch.

III

But now, newspapers
spread out on the ground,
rainbow awnings strung
up from the trees,

the picnic, a festival
of swimming, begins;
food taken, some half
awash in the frothy surf,

a few, up to their chins,
go through the motions
of swimming, their arms
a lazy mimic of the waves.

IV

But there, far out,
near the bigger, seagoing
fishing-boats at anchor,
one ambitious swimmer

shows off her skill.
Hair flashing as the sun
catches, already low,
on arms as on the water,

fish dart to her
and as if excited by her
presence, her performance—
no less than their habit

at this hour—frolic,
in pairs, sometimes
in schools that seem one
rainbowed curve, leap high

V

above her. Then
even as the day goes
down, sinking somewhere,
a molten treasure

at the bottom
of the sea, the swimmer,

‹ 127 ›

done with swimming,
by some artful strokes,

sure of herself
as of her course, returns
to shore. Whatever she
was after, as she stands,

dripping yet serene,
a last reflection, on
the sand, she has, for
a time at least, found it.

VI

So, night glinting
round in mottled waves,
two, swum far out, far in,
through one another's arms,

desire briefly routed,
drift upon the moon-
lit current before sleep.
And as the mind goes out,

exploring memories,
sensations like deposits
in the veins, the far-
out, lively places where

the body's lain, elations
gather, sun and wind
and water freshened, able
so, intrepid, to remain.

❖ ❖ ✦ ❖ ❖

Pasternak and Ivanov:
Translations, Adaptations,
Associations

«1968–77»

❖ ❖ ✦ ❖ ❖

«BORIS PASTERNAK»

The Breakup

I

O two-tongued angel, on my grief a hundred
proof no less I should have got you drunk.
But I'm not one, whatever pain the lies encouraged
from the start, to claim a tooth for a tooth.
And now the clever, festering doom!

Oh, no, betraying angel, it's not fatal,
not this suffering, this rash of the heart.
But why at parting shower me with such a rain
of blows to the body? Why this pointless
hurricane of kisses? Why, your mockery
supreme, kill me in everybody's sight?

II

O shame, how overwhelming you can be!
Yet at this breaking-up how many dreams persist.
Were I no more than a jumbled heap
of brows and eyes and lips, cheeks, shoulders, wrists,

‹ 131 ›

for my grief so strong, forever young,
at the order of my verse, its ruthless march,
I would submit to those and, leading them
in battle, storm your citadel, O monstrous shame.

III

All my thoughts I now distract from you,
if not at parties, drinking wine, then in heaven!
Surely one day, as the landlord's next door bell
is ringing, for someone that door will open.

I'll rush in on them in tinkling December, say,
the door pushed wide—and here I am, far as the hall!
"Where've you come from? What's being said?
Tell us the news, the latest scandal from the city."

Is all my grief mistaken?
Will it mutter later, "She mirrored her exactly,"
as, gathering myself for a leap past forty feet,
I burst out crying, "Is it really you?"

And the public squares, will they spare me?
Ah, if you could only know what pain I feel
when, at least a hundred times a day, the streets,
amazed, confront me with their counterfeits of you.

IV

Go ahead, try to stop me, try to put out
this fiery fit of sorrow, soaring
like mercury in a barometer.
Stop me from raving about you. Don't be ashamed,
we are alone. Turn out the lights, turn them
out, and douse my fire with fire.

V

Like combers twine this cloudburst of cold elbows,
like lilies, silken-stalwart, helpless palms.
Sound the triumph! Break loose! Set to! In this wild race
the woods are roaring, choked on the echo of Calydonian
    hunts,
where Acteon pursued Atalanta like a doe to the clearing,
where in endless azure, hissing past the horses' ears,
they kissed and kissed to the uproarious baying of the chase,
caressed among the shrillest horns and crackling trees,
the clattering hoofs and claws.
Like those break loose, break loose, rush into the woods!

VI

So you're disappointed? You think we should
part with a swan song for requiem,
with a show of sorrow, tears showering
from your eyes dilated, trying their victorious power?

As if during mass the frescoes, shaken by what's playing
on Johann Sebastian's lips, were to tumble from the arches!
From this night on in everything my hatred discovers
a dragging on and on that ought to have a whip.

In the dark, instantly, without a thought
my hatred decides that it is time
to plough it all up, that suicide's folly
slow, too slow, the speed of a snail.

VII

My love, my angel, just as in that night
flying from Bergen to the Pole, the wild geese

‹ 133 ›

swooping, a snowstorm of warmest down, I swear,
O Sweet, my will's not crossed when I urge you,
Dearest, please forget and go to sleep.

When like a Norwegian whaler's wreck, to its stock ice-
    jammed,
a winter's apparition, rigid past its masts, I soar,
fluttered in your eyes' aurora borealis, sleep, don't cry:
all before your wedding day will heal, my dear.

When like the North itself beyond the outmost settlements,
hidden from the arctic and its ice floe wide awake,
rinsing the eyes of blinded seals with midnight's rim,
I say—don't rub your eyes, sleep, forget—it's all nonsense.

VIII

My table's not so wide that, pressing my chest
against its board, I cannot crook my elbow
round the edge of anguish, those straits
of countless miles, quarried by "Farewell."

(It's night there now) Ah, to have your cloudy hair
(They've gone to sleep) the kingdom of your shoulders!
(All lights are out) I'd return them in the morning,
and the porch would greet them with a nodding branch.

O shield me, not with flakes, but with your hands,
pain's ten sufficient fingers, the spikes
of winter stars, like the placards of delay
posted on trains northbound into blizzards!

IX

The trembling piano licks foam from its lips.
This delirium, tossing, will strike you down.

You murmur, "Dearest!" "No!" I cry back. "Never
in the midst of music!" And yet how could we be closer

than in the twilight here, the score like a diary,
page after page, year after year, tossed on the fire.
O wondrous memories that, luring us still,
astonish the spirit! But you are free.

I shan't keep you. Go on. Give yourself to others.
Leave at once. Werther's already had his day.
But now the air itself reeks death:
opening a window is like opening a vein.

Illness

At dusk you appear, a schoolgirl still,
a schoolgirl. Winter. The sunset a woodsman hacking
in the forest of hours. I lie back to wait for dusk.
At once we're hallooing; back and forth we call.

But the night! A torture chamber, bustling hell.
Come—if anything could bring you!—see for yourself.
Night's your flitting away, your engagement, wedding,
last proceedings of a hangman's court against me.

Do you remember that life, the flakes like doves
in flock thrusting their breasts against the howling
and, the tempest swirling them, fiendishly
dashed to the pavements?

You ran across the street, winds billowing under us,
a flying carpet—sleds, cries, crystals headlong!

For life, inspired by the blizzard, gushed
like blood into a crimson cloud.

Do you remember that moment, the hawkers,
the tents, the jostling crowd, the coins a puppy's
moist nose? Those bells, encumbered by snow,
do you remember their grumbling before the holidays?

Alas, love, I must summon it all.
What can replace you? Pills? Patent medicines?
Frightened by my bottomless insomnia, sweat-soaked,
I look sideways from my pillow as with a horse's eye.

At dusk you appear, still taking exams.
It's recess: robins flutter, headaches, textbooks.
But at night how they clamor for thirst, how glaring
their eyes, the aspirins, the medicine bottles.

« SUITE FOR BORIS PASTERNAK »

Originally, at Mrs. Olga Carlisle's suggestion, I translated as faithfully as I could a group of Pasternak poems. And I thought I was done with Pasternak and translating. But then I turned for comparison's sake to already published renderings of his work. And as I read poems past the ones I had attempted, a desire to release the fundamental impulse I felt lurking in a number of them prompted the following suite. Only one poem, "Malady," grew directly out of my earlier work with Mrs. Carlisle; once I had finished "Illness" I tried a freer version of it.

A Russian Lesson

I

Hunched over your pages,
I tighten my eyes as though
I might, through the pitchblack
of this language I don't know,
via the tracks
            you've left

in it, benighted as I am,
by concentration penetrate
the swirling sheets on sheets;
such struggling
                    seems just
right, the very core of poetry-
making and something you, sitting
deep inside your Russian
winter, must have understood.

Others, hearing, would scoff,
as your time in its frenzy
hounded you: a grown man, playing
with words no one can understand
while the world is burning!

Oh it was terribly hard on you,
hard as on our Hawthorne say,
hiding away in his mother's house,
scorn noisy in his mind, haunted
by the living
                    as by the dead,
the piratical and the proud,
so unbowed by the ruthless fates
they seemed to push them past
themselves
                    as into his thoughts
till he was scarcely sure
he had not, like the creatures
he had long pursued, turned
into a ghost and disappeared.

II

But I have you to keep me
company; even in my feeling

‹ 138 ›

lost inside this rigid winter's
black-and-white, as through
the reaches
                of time and death
you've gone into, I count
on you. With your old peasant
women, workers, students, country-
men you've come to stay.

The light you shed like a lamp
in a distant room, shadowing
long, frozen lanes, and the light
things cast out of themselves,
glowing in your words,
                                flow
over me. That light reflects
something, a bounty, of forest-
deep firs, lining your house,
snows too,
                falling through them
as through bottomless space,
and in the field across the road
the little cemetery, snug
in blue-bright wooden fences

with zigzag crosses, planted
in the snow, and rose-petaled
paperflowers, children flashing
beyond it as they swish by
on a pond.
                I count on such gifts,
your great anguish and your loving-
kindness, reaching out, to see
me through, to help me find
you.

III

And this that follows,
a wreath composed of leaves
gathered from your rare garden,
trimmed as I transplant them,
is where we most meet.
                    For
having seen what those who hated
and feared, as well as those
who thought they admired, did
to you,
            catching glimpses of
your sad face through the barbed
wire of translations, I know
that till I try, by giving
whatever love and skill
                    I have,
to let you be in your own poems,
but as they come alive in me
and claim as they release this
larger life,
            you cannot be—
nor I with you—triumphant, free.

Malady

Quicker than the inquisition's night-
sly agents, than the secret police
pounced on you, trussed up, gagging,
this oppression, raging, spirits you away.

A gleam on the night, intent
as watching at your window, while
the ice keeps concentrating. A something
ghostly, fever in furs, the muttering

clock enfleshed, creaks on and on
precisely. Translated into you, the poker
helping and the creepy fire, the many-
dayed, lunatic-raving, all-out blizzard.

The dark like shiny, caked-up ice
lies still. Palings lap the starlight,
creamy among fir-trees, stuck, peeled
sticks, in midnight's fathomless well.

But now the blind snow shuffles
the firs, pawing the air like a cat.
A flickering follows, candles walking,
a phlegmy cough as of a throat long dead.

In this tree-hollow nesting hollows,
sky squinting through, the telegraph
lines, despite the echoing "answer me!,"
as they would spell out phrases sputter.

Twigs and needles gouge all hearing,
the sphere-hung spaces bundle silence.
Perhaps the flickering's the only answer
to someone's frantic "who's there?"

A gleam on the night, intent
as watching at your window, while
the ice keeps concentrating. A something
in furs, cracked record needle-caught.

And biting your lips till they are
white, snow-white, as your face locked
in your hands. Let those come after
read this storm with storms of wonder.

November Late

We've gone through two thirds
of the house by now, and what
we've left behind, a jumble
of junk, we cannot push
back through.
                  Soon the walls
will topple, ashes flying,
and a wind, so inconsolable
there is no arguing with;
it snatches
            every bit
of breath. And light, just
enough, will rise, a raw-
edged morning like a wound,
to see
            what wretchedness
is here, what howling
emptiness. Light or not,
who's to tell these chills
from fever?
            This chatter,
gaunt as hunger's self, grinds
down everything that happens

in its way. The animals,
pulling the holes
              in after,
whimpering, scrounge and bury
themselves many times over
in rank sleep. The tree
trunks sprawl
             like timber
gnawed and left by fire
after it has had its fill.
Some hectic, feverish to tear
the world and itself to pieces,
seems about to have its will.

"Fresh Paint"

"Fresh paint?" I took that sign
to be an invitation. Certainly,
clumsy as I was for looking more
closely, it rubbed off on me,

on hands and face and deeper
still, as though my breath
kept brushing it in and freshly,
my eyes also, the lashes stroking

away, as though to paint you
forever, over and over, banked
and stoked beneath these lids,
that sleep shone with the look

of you, the young moon blinking,
darkness too, as soon as you were
gone, the gloom of me, as though,
lightning-struck, it stuck.

Now I shudder to think of new
events, of seasons yet to be
(at best they're fall). All seem
to come to spread that shade,

deep-dyed, relentlessly fresh.
Who'd have thought I was meant—
and eagerly chose—to be the un-
paid sorcerer's apprentice!

Sultry Dawn

In coos a pigeon's measuring
out the morning at your window.
And fallen wash from a broken
line, bedraggled faded sleeves,
some branches sprawl in troughs
and gutters. A haze
and sputter as of a fetid,
snoring breath. Clouds over it,
yet low and luring me
like trinkets in a hawker's tray
or in a fair the prizes passing
of a lottery. And as I watch,
dawn behind them like a washer-

woman's ruddy cheeks and breast,
washerwoman too the blather
in the bushes.
                    Again I strain
hoping to overhear the song
splashed from your pitcher,
your lips dipped in it, flashing
still, your new-washed glances,
nimble fingers warming as you
wake your nodding mirror.
But the noise instead
as of a brawl burst round,
the rowdy clouds, the blather
in the bushes.
                    Oh I wished
with all my might the racket
stop and sleep at least return.
The fair was on, the crowds
come rushing. The stink,
the heat is all, the pushing.
In great disgust you have
retreated far behind your shade-
                    drawn window.

A Poem Recalled

Even as I dream of home again,
the huddled rooms at dusk grown large
with sadness and with ghostly crowds,
I'm there, taking off my overcoat,

and as I pierce the thin partitions,
no stray beam subtler, binding images,
I find some comfort in the street-
lights ebbing and flowing below.

Again the houses and the trees, sighing
chorally, repeat their common, fragrant
story. And everywhere old hoary winter
sternly busy with her tidying up.

Again at dinner-time the night
swoops down, like gangsters skulking
out of darkened doorways, gypsies, spooks,
to overwhelm the alleys, much confused.

Again, O City, weak as I may feel,
I listen to you and match my phrases
to your smoking, smells and noises,
to your giant building going on.

This way, for the sake of furious days
rushing down on us, I yoke myself to you
that you may know our past by heart,
know me as well, a poem recalled.

Inside the Storm

As I go prowling through room
after room there's no one here
but shadowy twilight and winter,
winter like a prisoner panting,
maddened to escape, clutching
at the drawn-tight curtains.

And below nothing but that shivering
cold, blowing up scraps of paper
and the snow on snow, nothing
but row on row of roofs
and, like a feverish, unblinking
image in a dream, of snow.

The night's hoarfrost reports
in writing large and crackling-clear
the winter storms now hustling up,
conflicts kept on ice in them
and last year's grief, too monstrous
then for us or only one time's air.

Remorse and blame stoke on
and on within my smoky heart.
Still hungry cold, not satisfied
by this, nor by my sighs that
keep an ember burning in my brain,
pulls down the sagging window-frames.

But then the doorway's drape
begins to shake as though with all
that once passed in, passed out
forever. But no, the gust that parts
it like a fervor pure enough to be
the future means you entering.

There you will stand, poised
by the doorway, twilight turning,
winter too, amazed, you in something
white and simple, white and simple
as a snowflake, the last to come
that, topping, stops the snow.

From A to Z

At last you've come, sharing
this same air with me, as near
as our Kiev, leaning, peering in,
a sultry glance, through the window.

Kiev, struggling in its sleep,
its will indomitable, to tear
the stifling, silk-sly collar, falling,
brick by brick, from off its neck.

Kiev, sweating among its leaves,
out at last, larking with the poplars
along its exultant avenues that first
had straggled here, a mob worn-out.

You think and glide like our Dnieper,
sporting greenest paths and groves;
my book sprouted out of secret roots,
day by day you turn up its prize entries.

So now you bid me sit by you,
and totally engrossed, with fixed looks
going over you from A to Z,
I strive to copy you into my book.

A Summer Thunderstorm

Rinsed and flooded, flooded
through and through, the way

a wind is filtered as it blows
across the Hudson and then
through giant trees in clumps
and finally through the corn
at harvest.
        Flooded, rinsed
and cleansed by the summer
thunderstorm, the lightning
gleaming on the rain,
the rain a shuddering white
host of tiny, jagged lightnings,
a mirror's bits,
                the world,
the trees astare, the bushes
crouching, birds with skirts
flipped over their heads.
I felt the negatives developing
at once, as clear as day,
inside the deepest corners

of my mind; mercurial
the light that plays through
me, the sun at best caught
in this night, in waves
a hundred, hundred snapshots
leafed through me. And then
a heady fragrance
                as of wine
pressed from the sodden dust,
the tracks within the grass,
and water spouting at each
gutter, eager to report
what rousing, ravishing events
it's just passed through.

Blithewood

Like surveyors with their shiny, crystal
tools, precision instruments, the rain moved
through this clearing. Now their lines
connect the drooping lilies of the valley.

And dazzle thunders in the mullein's fuzzy ears.
The first dews dangle from their lobes.
Exclusive as ladies of high tone they scorn
to mingle their expensive, far-fetched scents.

As evening tea is clattering in the garden,
the mosquito's sails puffed up with mistiness,
night, relaxed in silky dark among the pansies,
randomly plinking a strung-taut guitar,

the world relents with dusky violets:
years and faces throng the mind. And thoughts.
Each thing the deft surveyors, understanding
fate, reclaim and order for the future.

This Gray Age

Had I known it then, really known,
before I began this wretched scribbling
(my dear friend, older in the business,
even as he was about to leave the stage
forever, did his best to warn me;
but how, caught up in that dream, fame
and its glamor, could I understand him),

known how deadly the lines of passion,
clutching at the throat, would be,

I would most certainly have scorned
all this desperate fiddle, this dressing
up my feelings, I all absorbed, in high-
falutin craft. One fumbles away at first,
hardly aware of the price he has,
in effort as in fevered pain, to pay.

But now the act is done. Instead
of gags and jugglery, glib cleverness
that hogs the stage a moment, this gray
age like Rome, bored with mere sideshows,
wooden daggers, bags of spouting
pig-blood, cries out for the real thing—
that the actor, falling in earnest, die.

When passion is the play, play,
alas, is over, and the one who long
had sought the spotlight, in it at last,
finds to his astonishment that he's
not mouthing art, the phrases he's put
through their measured paces a thousand,
thousand times, but the fatal, final lines
of earth itself, life, destiny unbudgeable.

To Anna Akhmátova

§ (and to Boris Pasternak, who wrote it first)

Just thinking of you—such is your power—
spurs me on to find the appropriate words.

Mistakes? Perhaps. But who can call them that
as long as I am faithful to my feelings?

The myriad clatter on the soaking roofs,
the boardwalks' tiptoed, echoing bucolic
harmonize with a certain city emerging
in every verse, in every syllable reverberant.

Despite spring's overwhelming tides,
muddy roads balk passage like your customers.
Crouched over piles of work, the sunset sears;
eyes blear, bloodshot, stitching by a lamp.

You hunger for the openness of Ladoga
and, worn out, hurry to the lake for rest
and change. In vain. The canals smell fusty
as years-locked, dank, bulging closets.

Like a hollow walnut shell the hot wind
frets their waves, the blinking lids as well
of stars, branches, lamp-posts, lights, one
lonely seamstress peering far beyond the bridge.

In unity as in definition eyes,
like objects, vastly differ; yet the sky
at night, scored by the glancing polar gleam,
exerts the purest power, melting fright.

So I conjure up your face, your glance.
Not the image of that pillar of salt inspires
me by which five years ago your meters
fixed our fear of looking back,

but one that lives in all your early work
where bits of unremitting truth prevailed.
Now in everything, like wires shooting sparks,
your poems hum with our precious past.

« GEORGY IVANOV »

"Thank god there is no Tsar"

Thank god there is no Tsar
Thank god there is no Russia
Thank god there is no God,

Only a jaundiced twilight
Only hoary stars
Only illimitable years.

Thank god there is no one
Thank god there is nothing
So dark, so dead
It could not be deader
Shall never be darker,
No one able to help us
And no need to help.

"Sleeping, he saw Ophelia in his dream"

Sleeping, he saw Ophelia in his dream
Swamp lights around her, nuptial mists

Like a musical spiral she drifted
Mirrors dreamlike reflecting her

Like a nimbus fireflies surrounded her
Like a forest cornflowers sprang up in her wake

How casual it is to suffer! You can surrender your soul
And still be unable to transmit a dream
And knowing that disaster stands at your back
To yearn for no one, to dream of nothing

"The affair was badly flawed"

The affair was badly flawed
Yet even so life opened
In the mist her misty eyes
Her double, swan-wide wings

And even so shadows flittered
While the candle spluttered
Even so strings twangled
Sounding their pointless happiness.

"That pointless happiness,
was it worth it?"

That pointless happiness, was it worth it?
It being, notwithstanding, possible? O certainly.
And it fluttered off into the emerald sky
Where the evening star is sparkling.

Be more gullible, frivolous, bold!
If you cannot sleep, contrive some dreams.
Be, if you can, one with the evening star:
Just as dazzling, just as cold.

"Losing yourself in thought,
daydreaming"

Losing yourself in thought, daydreaming,
Your rod begins to quiver in your hand
And here's the golden minnow
On the silver hook.

It's so spontaneous, so winsome:
The sun, the wind, the water.
Even the fish feels choked in its stream
Even it requires bad luck

The sky to be struck out,
The boat to fondle the water,

The butter to start sizzling
Gently in the frying pan

"Mirrors, reflecting each other"

I

Mirrors, reflecting each other,
Mutually distort their reflections.

I've faith not in the invincibility of evil,
But only in the inevitability of defeat,

Not in the music that scorched my life,
But in the ashes the scorching left.

II

A game of fate. A game of good and evil.
A game of wits. Imagination's game.

"Mirrors, reflecting each other,
Mutually distort their reflections,"

They assure me: you've won the game!
It hardly matters, I no longer play.

It's true the poet in me may not die,
But the man in me is dying abundantly.

‹ 156 ›

FROM

The World Before Us

«1970»

Pleasure, Pleasure

And watching Hoppy curled up
in my lap, the way he goes
purring under my hand into sleep,
this watching is a pleasure.

A pleasure too Renée
in the next room practicing
the violin, going over the same
tracks again and again, trying

the notes like doors
to stores more and more open
for business, like stars lighting
up some Persian night asleep

under the skin of day.
Is a pleasure and a pleasure
this friend and that, a light
of one color and another,

not only to read
by as the world takes shape,
the sea rolled over like Hoppy
in a rapture of churning,

but a light
that is also the thing lit,

the world in its juicy, joyous
particulars. And outside the day

in each leaf now
is lighting, each leaf by its own
lights, maple first, then sumac,
inspired but responding

as it must. Already
the year is more than half way
here, to be followed by snow,
at first hesitant midair,

going up and then,
to go farther, down in a very
ecstasy of windy cold. Pleasure,
pleasure and the darkest light.

The Heir Apparent

My father's ripped pants,
my grandfather's bulging shoes.
Get used to the patch that covers
the seat of one, his knees
stuffed out with prayers and a kind
of crawling, tight, tight, on a proud man.

And bundle the toes
for those miles of walking
factory floors that turn the world
into one tiny spot with girls
at machines like machines until
his satchels, bursting, spouted trinkets,

ribbons to prank
a country fair. And hair
spun out of the web of my mother,
hair like a nest hatching eggs
of her anger igniting each other,
a desert ensuring the eggs' eggs' future.

And plying them all,
bright threads on a loom,
playing them out, then pulling
them taut and, having bitten
off frayed ends, knotting them in,
my grandmother who never admitted

America, lived in it
as she had lived in Warsaw
and traveled over the dizzy sea:
a few familiar rooms, jammed
with bodies lurched against each other,
only she swept good space among.

I jostled by these
and the many nameless, my walk
a bit cramped for the bunioned shoes,
the baggy knees, the hair full of snarls,
but my grandmother tidying up, serving
cups of hot tea. With lemon.

"Yes, But . . ."
for WCW again

There he was—having spent
the night with us, the first

time away from home alone,
terribly frail for another stroke,
his dreams still shaking him—
his fame steadily leaping ahead,

and he complaining to me,
struggling just to be somebody,
expecting me to comfort him!

Manfully, if with a bitter sense
of injustice, I did my best:
"Why, Bill, you've left a good
green swath of writing behind you."

And he, in a low voice,
most mournfully, "Yes, but
is it poetry?"
                        That years ago.
Only now I begin to understand
the doubts necessary to one
always open, always desperate
(his work's honesty, spontaneity—
work nothing, life—depended
on it),
            one too so given
over to the moment, so lover-
faithfully serving it,
he could remember or believe
in little else.
                        (Some months
later Frost would visit,
older, sturdy as an ancient oak,
unlike Williams, who could not read
to the end of a verse,
                        intoning
his poems well over an hour

‹ 162 ›

with tremendous relish, then
standing on his solid stumps
another hour batting it out
with students,
                no doubts shaking
him and few new leaves breaking
out of him.)
                And only now,
the years, the doubts accumulating,
can I be grateful to Bill
for his uncertainty,
                can I lean
on it, lean more than on all
his accomplishments, those greeny
asphodel triumphs.

The Youngest Son

Cast out among your impatient,
scornful elders, the oldest a scholar
hunched over his books in several languages
before you learned to say "Sorry";

the second quick, clever,
finding your clumsiness like dirt
all over your body; and your many sisters,
grim, raw, willed like jealous men.

With your wiry little father
always a smouldering fire, a single
word enough to flare him forth, exacting
instantaneous obedience from his stiff brood,

treating you like some mistake
his wife unforgivably had made. Soon
you learned the skills of skulking, stealing,
hiding. Knuckled words, blows

aimed at one's weaknesses,
mold one as well as any other lesson.
You became, perfect, exactly what they said
you were: a cheat, a thief, a liar.

And yet they found you
useful for the minor, dingy chores.
You brought in water and wood, swept floors,
carried messages, often those

most revealing since they
hardly cared about your knowing.
Maybe it was then you started, broom in hand
and shears, some flowers, of a Sunday

to take care of the family
plot, tending graves of brothers
and sisters who had barely lived, some dying
many years before your birth.

Then, grown-up, you went
about your business, from one job
and trouble to another, your second brother
bailing you out exasperatedly,

the whole family meeting
to recount your failures or, worse,
to sit over you in hourslong, noisy silence.
Still no matter how far

you wandered you could not
let them go. And reluctantly they

grew used to your dependence, the weakness
natural to such a ne'er-do-well.

Now age has come upon them.
The oldest, more stooped than ever,
recognizes no one. Only you can reach him,
feed him; only you are there

below his books. And one
by one they turn to you, efficient—
for the arts you've learned—in the larger,
necessary chores. You, the cheat,

the thief, the liar,
come of age at last. The training
they were all so set on giving you now works
splendidly. And you move among them.

Having been a child of trouble
all your life, you take the family over.

The Last Letters,

whether they be followed
by what we call a natural death
or suicide, tend to be the most engrossing,

a kind of undressing
so complete nothing else possibly compares.
Leant closer, squinting at the lines,

we have the sense that
we are drawing near to something
ultimate: whatever the force of the occasion,

and the affectations,
not to say disingenuousness, death may induce,
a man, precisely as he turns

his back on what
he has been thirty years or seventy, is bound
to tell the truth. And turns his back

on the future also.
Not all its promises can make him wait;
what he's in for, he now sees, can only worsen,

deprivation, emptiness,
worst if he's been happy. And even if nothing
more than nothing should ensue,

the void ("he took his dog
for its evening walk, then shot
his brains out" or "she set out her rare plant

to catch the rain,
made several phone calls, downed
an overdose of pills"), something must crackle

over that last broken line,
something, we cannot help feeling,
from the other side of that life even as it is

being consumed,
even as it consumes itself forever
in its own private flame, now breaking loose,

like some great moth
throwing itself into the fire
which is itself to enlarge it, but lost to it

in the very moment of having.
And most of all if it is someone who has been
a master. As we say, a great gift,

gifts he finally admits
no help to him, a burden rather.
And, much worse than that, a terrible taunting.

As if to say we as well,
whatever admiration we may have felt for him,
did not find his gifts enough.
                              Not till now.

A Certain Village

Once in late summer,
the road already deep in twilight,
mixing colors with some straggly
wildflowers, I came to a village
I did not know was there
                              until
I stepped into its narrow street.
Admiring the prim, white houses
nestled among their veteran,
lofty trees,
            I found myself in
a tiny square with a little dawdl-
ing fountain and a rickety tower,
its owlish clock absentmindedly
counting minutes now and then.

And in the fountain the face
of morning seemed to linger as
though searching. The air was fresh,
breathing out the fragrances
of a recent shower.
     I luxuriated
in my senses, like meeting
unexpectedly a pack of friends
years and years unthought of, laden
with all kinds of gifts.
     Then
as I stopped to knock at the door
of a house that had seemed occupied
with happy noises, a silence
fell on it,
    the light went out—
and was it instant eyes like flakes,
ten thousand, thousand flakes,
and all unknowing, flurried
round me?
    Wherever I turned
I was met by the unmistakable
accusation, "Stranger!" I, who had,
I thought, begun here and who now
required lodgings
     for the night,
was denied and from the start.

FROM

Fireweeds

«1976»

Ten Little Rembrandts

There, with ten Rembrandts
or so, he slumped in the corner
like a sloppy janitor, an ex-sexton
in a corner of heaven, one eye opening
to say with a sigh as the bustle
flutters by him, "God again!"

So you speak with uneasy,
loving regret of Paris: "I do love it
but never feel comfortable in it.
And this time I gave it ten days.
But then the Parisians don't seem
much at home in it either.

The Louvre with its ages on ages
of dust, rooms empty, and the room
with ten little Rembrandts, and that
crumpled old guard snoring away
in one corner! Well, I flew back
home soon after, and almost at once

the whole trip, the cities,
their people, pictures, plays
became little more than a jumble
of names. But I assure myself
that each did something, is doing now,
and will go on doing. Who knows."

So you remind me of another
brooding on the Brooklyn lectures,
one in particular of a famous writer,
she heard in her youth: "A Russ
he must have been, enflamed
about the havoc that had plagued

his world, its scars long
after visible, about the dead
there seemed not earth, not mind
and time, enough to bury. But I can't
remember anything any more. No, not
the speaker's name or even some

one quirk he may have had.
But I keep hoping that all that
got into me and is working still."
All that, like ten little Rembrandts
hard at work, in the mighty space
of our forgetting exerting wily wills.

Off to Patagonia
for Pili

Say it's an important event like this:
a famous foreign dignitary about to arrive
or the government planning an excursion,
a messenger announcing it or a newspaper
dispatch (by now a rumor should do,
a clouding over of the day), and those
under suspicion without a sigh pack a bag,

kiss the family good-bye and for the duration
take themselves off to prison.

It had become a way of life.
But that's the way life was in Spain.
And no doubt countless other lands as well.
When you were a schoolgirl you had this mad
highschool Latin professor who, arranging
the class in two straight rows, kept
the rear section of the classroom clear.
And if anyone of you failed to answer
as he liked, pointing imperiously

to that demarked, empty zone,
he said: "Off to Patagonia with you!"
The Latin you had learned? Forget it!
But you did master something: grammar,
punctuation, syntax of a basic sort that,
whether you realize it or not, now stands
you in good stead. The time, standard
Spanish time, comes when it comes,
and then—for less than a word,

an imperceptible lurch in the day,
you and your life suddenly grown thin—
it says: "Off to Patagonia with you!"
And you, packing a bag, kiss the family
good-bye and for the duration disappear
into that prison, promptly clanking
shut. And there you wait patiently,
stern as the treatment is, doing your best
to remember that, so far, you have returned.

‹ 173 ›

Another and Another and . . .

. . . to go on living after all.—Odysseus

Even the liveliest of us had
to regale himself with farfetched
lives he had not lived, spontaneous
roles, spun out with plots, inspired
complications, accidents, seafaring,
like the spumy wonders that his wife
aggrandized daily from her hands.

It must have refreshed him
for a moment to shed his briny,
pounded body, habits of a lifetime,
tugging always, nagging at him,
like the gods, fate he must follow,
for its daily due, allowing never
one digression from its course.

But given the space, a new
world waiting—charged though
it might be with trials, dangers—
of a stranger's eyes and ears,
stage like no other to frisk on,
apt for any fantastical performance,
he could assume a mask, that role
lighter than feathers with wings

working them: a name, names
made of breath alone, and deeds
to stroll in like a god, the same
daring, the same freedom. And those
eyes, sparkling their amazement,
mounted snowy peaks upon his words,
composed—those ears—a music balmy
round him birds might loll in,

glad to add, to drown in,
their own most luxuriant songs.
For a moment, far past all that he
had done, was yet in ways unknown
to him to do, he was free to wander
the way—lighthearted, true—of his
own wish, to do the things he was
not meant to. And by feigning so,

his acting another and another and . . . ,
he became that much more himself.

The Storeroom

I

So many things
at her—day after day those madly blooming
things, crammed into tiny, rocky Ithaca,
a bare exposure in the sun—no wonder
the storeroom's twilit cool entices her.

Where else, long years of yearning worked,
close-figured, into yarn, the suitors crowding,
more and more suspicious, round her loom?

And there, the ruses, every hard choice, shed,
absorbed as if by her dream-riddled sleep,
she stands.
            At first the shapes seem satisfied
to keep the dark. But glimmers of them gather,
and in huddled companies, then one

‹ 175 ›

by one they press toward her:
        an axhead,
 scythes, lump bronze, lump gold,
 piled under, earth and earth's
 before the race began,
       restoring
 her to a time the mind was not yet
 here to trouble, time itself
 of small account,
       and to a time
 washed, fired, over both of them,
 but lovely-slow, the world not yet
 intruding.
     Hung next to the scythes,
 his longbow, shadowed as if by
 offshoots at their feathery, light-
 shafted darting.
      In the corner
 just below, bow's echoing, a lyre
 leant, slack with its music
 drowsing.
     And beyond them, sagged
 from sweat-black, ragged thongs,
 his cuirass.
     Her fingers carefully
trace dents in it. At once, air heaving,
uneven throbbings thrill her fingertips.

II

Like bugs flying, beams flit around her.
Strayed through slits, attracted to each self-
lit thing, what are they if not his goddess
never blinking?
     There, as though the grey-
eyed sea had fixed its gaze, Athene stands,

her favorite beside her.
      And her glance,
igniting his, strikes studded bucklers,
spears racked up.
       Instantly the room
one ricochet, he's plunged into the clash,
yet stayed by each thing in its sovereignty.

The glare too strong, his wife looks away
to a deep-bellied crater.
       The country glow
it basks in, brimming like a wine, pours
over on a polished chest.
       Opening it,
she fondles tunics she had woven, thinner
than dried onion skins; a shining, long
collected in the dark, erupts,
         sly movements
of a body like a soft breeze in them still.

And shadows step, diaphanous and supple,
forth.
    Step too as from the man-sized urn
a flock in flight encircles, and wildflowers,
whirling over dryads, satyrs, beaten
that they seem to cry, their bodies writhing,
rapture.
     Startled by her glance,
     the urn revolves each daedal
     side:
       fat summer preening
     first; then swiftly turning
     colors; paling
        into rigid
     winter, mounds like eyesight
     banked,

        night underscoring
   as it threatens, by it death
   pitch-bright.

III

           But there, just outside,
the land he, never letting go, is blind to
till the goddess hail him down to earth.

New crops rotted on old, the vineyards
slumped within a drunken buzz, the suitors
swarm, retainers and the women servants
waiting on their appetites.
                Once luminous,
each dawn delighting like a bright-eyed child
to gawk among the loveliness, rooms now
one trough awash with swill.
                And by the house's
gaping doors his sheep and cattle mired
down except as they are turning, turning
on a spit.
        The trees, their untrimmed limbs
a flotsam many seasons, steep in leaves
like someone lazily drifting.
                Drifting
geese and drowsing drakes, but often flurried
into squawky storms by wild curs, sure
to rend him should he return.
                Only one
old hound slumps peacefully. Long worlds ago
gold fleece to morning.
                A party hurrying
by, aimed at the shimmering grove, the horns,
the hallooings hovered over, much as August
breezes fail to rouse the dog.

‹ 178 ›

But then,
like that beggar dumped on steaming dung,
sunk in a dream, a sting abruptly at it
out of streaming afternoon—
                    is it a sparkle
from some leaf-and-shadow-speckled chase,
a boar's tusk slashing in, or merely one
of its abundant kin, the sizzling fleas?—
it recollects:
                    at once love's piercing blow
shatters its tough heart.
                    And weeping bitterly
among the gnarled, hard-bearing pear and fig,
his father, like that beggar beaked by suffering,
its whole flock which, nestled in him, spawns.

The son, a sapling, hardly grown enough
to master his estate, so let the arrow,
pacing its ravenous covey, loose.

        IV

                    Best of all,
his wife, loving the old man for the memories,
the miseries, they share, as for his own
which, though unknown to her, reverberate.

She, catching in her son's eye glimpses,
always nearer, of her husband, the wonder
which their mingling with the goddess flared
inside the hidden room, devises schemes
to save their world.
                    The hidden room?
Entering, she remarked a spider
neatly fasten filaments from bow
to lyre, chinked light gliding

on those lines,
              then link them
to the massive double doorpost,
though the door, each time
swung open, broke the web.

Never making, even if she could, her work
too finished lest the goddess, much offended,
end her world, but keeping death, the suitors,
dangled at arm's length.
              Kept them,
    like the captive figures
    flitted in the tapestry, alive.
                        She
this day, though squabbling as before filled
the house, resorting to her own becornered
yet commodious storeroom:
                    weaving;
                              then,
night come, a revelry swept up, unraveling
the fabric rippled on her warp.
                        Just so
    from moon's collaborating loom
    the nymphs play out—diversely dyed
    and buoyed with dappled creatures,
    ripened to the West Wind's breath—
    the sea.
              Beguiled—by weeping,
    sighs?—to interrupt their sport,
    they jostle round her whirring work
    and gape, their shadows purpling
    the thrum, at her elaborate design.

‹ 180 ›

V

The web
daily spreads the fabulous tales she's drunk
from suppliant lips, inspired by their need,
by gods greedy for such nectared songs,
drunk also from the mouth, mellifluous
and terrifying, of her dreams:
                        steeds,
    hard tugging at the stitches
    to run in harness with the coursers
    of the sun, a slowly galloping,
    one summer day:
                  and rumbled
    in (the clacking of her loom?),
    the lumbersome horse, turning
    into thread which draws it forth,

    forth armored men, the ten years
    blazing out,
               redoubtable deities
    emblazoned, for the immortality
    their moment blossoms no less
    glorious than the blown May
    fly,
      to swansdown women
    shying from her shuttle as
    from centaurs:
              strewn wreckage
    when the day's light settles—
    bits of limbs, a jetsam glance—
    as if smoky Troy:
             then crises
    quaking in the woof, each sea-
    and landscape of his peril, rocks
    sticking out, tide-sucking monsters,
    silky trap a minor spirit spins.

Gladly she snaps threads.
                         But such exploits,
though every night nipped with the sun,
next day transformed as in the myths, for all
the life rammed into them still magnifying.

    VI

His wife who angles him upon her shining
line to haul him back—sometimes how he,
dragging, hangs on it, on her, the power
of her loneliness—from out that years-
bereaving, sea-and-wind-reeled tangle.

This shuttling, ceaseless, must chart out
his zigzag course; and stumbled on the clue
through her own maze, she carefully tracks him,
secreted in it, figure slow to show himself.

Must, as it keeps his crested helmet bobbing,
like his masted ship, above its element.

She, kindred to those spinsters never tired,
spider-canny, leaving just so much
each night, the narrow lifeline quivered
through her hands, for him to cling to.

    (And yet see how simple,
    blank even, though the sharpest
    needle guide it, each stitch
    seems to be;
            a stitch snarls:
    is it a sortie, far off going on,
    a battle waged and lost, his death?)

Strings, and heartstrings, twanging at his tug,
how can she hold him fast, that slippery one

a thousand twistings?
                    Her breath snags;
a stitch drops. Has he let go?
                        O, no,
not he, cliff-clinger, and most masterly
as castaway, afflictions gaping round him
in his craft.
            But still those ominous rifts
(recesses where, becalmed, and variously
bedded, he might recover in, might dis-
appear, so loved, forever?) moments when
she fails to find him under her fingers,
in her thoughts, her fears,
                        forgettings.

VII

Without him near, completing her, she feels
as much remote from home, confusion all
her once familiar things. Confusion all.

O for a time the giant space he'd filled,
his clamor claiming it, his urgent needs,
so emptied, pleased her; she could roam in it,
inviting, tasting, portions till now hidden
of herself.
            But soon the emptiness spoke out,
increasingly, as emptiness. For there
where his dear body used to be jag-ends
of her own.
            Hot tears crash over her,
tears would sweep him home, but these she fears—
his enemy so strengthened—must confound him
more, hurl him against some rock-ribbed coast.

(And yet within its dish the water winks:
morning, perched once, singing, on the crag-

‹ 183 ›

like shoulder?)
So his name repeated, sputtered
like a torch, should lighten every furtive nook,
but sighed, its syllables, to her dank pillow,
crumbles into air, winds rushing through

(a gust of voices,
riotous,
the scamper,
ruffling moonlight).
Someone brings a strap
wrenched off in battle, insisting it belonged
to him, bloodstains of course pure Trojan.

Another with a flourish proffers, tarnished
for the bearer's scratchy gutturals—
yet her breath can burnish it—a scrap
of speech he hoarded from some far assembly:
breaking through like sunlit surf, patched
with mist, that loved voice, thundrous still.

And showering its words on them, parched
listeners enrapt, an April spray when kindly;
raging, flakes like fiery shafts sure-aimed.

Flakes, fiery now, but blown by many a gust,
confusion all, a witless storm: each thing,
the most familiar, drifts, roost for such
forgetting.

VIII

But does she not at times,
as if, having tied a knot into that web

‹ 184 ›

to hold it (so hold him), absentmindedly
drift too?
       For even she, days dawdling,
must admit sun's blandishments, a bubbling
pipe, or else an air that springs, surprising,
from her lips to waken in her aimless
gaiety.
       So, darkness near—the loom
bulked silent, empty, capable of all—
putting her hearing out, her sight a scarlet
thread stiff in it, she, adrift on fragrant
sheets, sails not so swift, is dozing off.

     From out the night-pressed summer
     fields, sighs mixed with hissing
     locusts and the husky breezes
     rubbing stalks, all the madly
     blooming things rush in on her.

     At once the salty god—her blood
     his wade—his hatred ever at tide
     for him she loves, churns round.

     His tempests swarming through
     her breath, the headboard satyrs,
     dryads (suitors, maids?), entwining,
     whip into a fury.
              Like a ship
assailed, her body quaking, she grips fast
the rooted olive-post he shaped.
                Must she
forever play, the restless moon at work,
fidelity, a statue's role? Attend that knot,
her breath's dead center?

                    Wanting, much as he,
to be enmeshed (much like that godly duo,
naked in the net of their own, however
let-loose, farfetched weaving, and the net
her art would settle on them).

        IX

                    Adrift,
distracted—
            much as he by the wine-
dark, huffing sea, by the exotic
sites, diversions there, awaiting
him, and, raced ahead, clamorous
to greet him, fame;
                    one appetite
waylaying him, another, blown
several times past home, his breath
the gust outstrips all, driving him
earthward—
                suitors, lusty eyes to dress
her shimmering in.
                    She in little having
what that Helen needed armies of,
a city's ruin, to highlight—that flush
on her she feigns her own!—her loveliness.

        X

And yet how speak of her as one distracted?
For, unlike that other, she, housekeeping
her whole lot, can ill afford to play
the prodigal. Forget the prudent lessons
he had taught her?
                    So many years, not growing
younger, less sure daily he'll return,

                    ‹ 186 ›

spurn them, the choicest of the islands?
Or spurn the here and now, the meant to be
lived, whatever shape it happens to take?

Rather wait and see who might emerge.
No certainty that, given time, some one
of them will not become a man—fledglings
hardly older than their son, shell sticking
to them still, can any spread wings yet?—
like him.
         (And what use eagles, lions,
         prowling on some foreign shore,
         or maggots' rapturous song? Better
         a lout, this ancient beggar even,
         travel stinking on him, blessings
         of survival.)
                  Let notes be sent each suitor,
promises by private messenger,
a bait priming their hopes to win
the gifts they think, once having wed,
to recover many times over.
                      Had he but seen
her craft at work, fluttering in and out,
inspired, on that loom!

   XI

                A sleight.
                    Can they,
appetites blinding them, egregious longings
that have helped her cunning dupe them,
dear, goose-fattened enemy, who unwittingly
had bade this be, the seamy warp essential
to her tapestry, spy him
                   emerging,
slowly and yet clearly as in her ever-

lasting dream?
           (The glinting intermittent
in the rain, as on her tears, is it
his buckler, look?
          A glinting
bunched into a hand on hers;
or merely the first warm touch—
she reaches, reaches, cannot touch—
of dawn, her own hand stretched
before, not yet reclaimed?

Her fingers, nimble at the loom,
the dark, to summon up the instant—
honey spurt that stings—fit man
of him, responsive to each whim,
her dream no less than day outwits.)

There she stands, a goosegirl tending her
flock, winsome however they compare
with Leda's swan, just waddled from the pond.

And as she throws them grain, delighting
in their greediness, an eagle, thing
of iron, fire, arrows down to scatter them
among her hot, moist sighs like thawing snow.

A hard thing, hard, to be long bound to, bound
yet driven.
        Most as he is iron.

   XII

                Iron though
that, fired to the utmost, can be loving,
tender.
       And when he takes light—light!—

‹ 188 ›

hold of her, under those extended talons
dove most godly, no, most human, tender,
to embrace her into flying clouds
cannot compete with.
                    And in a half-drowse—
O that it would come to that again!—
side by side, after the wine she has set
out for him, in the firelight watching,
like a drama nearly forgotten, fitful
snatches from their lives.
                    There catching
on the flames' far side a glimpse of those
not yet, and of that one straining, as he
used to in her tapestry, to overhear,
so weave into, their story.
                    Thus they might
live on, their exploits magnifying still,
in minds of men to be.
                    (He wandering
from town to town, dust coating him,
encountering tribes so far inland
they have no sense of ships, oar-
winged, his grappling with the sea;

then boredom, lotus-eaters, sprawled
in it, more passive than those he long
ago had met,
                    vast desert kingdoms
churning out mirages, making Scylla
and Charybdis mangy pets;
                              men so far
inland his words can hardly pierce.
Yet by its bitterness summoning,
to his surprise, the best in him,
even if ignored.
                    But not entirely.

‹ 189 ›

For he would make his way to solitary,
hungry shores, through solitary,
hungry men, from Ireland to Russia,
sail dazzling, homecome, in some
hidden inlets of America.)
                          Forgotten,
the occasions he, and she no less, have spent
most of their lives on?
                          Never forgotten,
however she forgive.
                          So much of him,
the glamorous stranger, to be uncovered,
so much to step forth from the shadows,
supple, diaphanous, she will not judge,
not till she's heard the complicated story
out from his own lips.

    XIII

                          And yet can she,
her look coupling with his, endure the battle-
like blaze, the ricochet:
                          a thousand eyes
of men and monsters glanced from him, the grey-
eyed goddess, summoned by his gesture, women
also plucked, a nosegay;
                          in his hand,
soft yet fierce, the ram he gripped, and striplings
doomed;
        Troy's flames, and Helen's, flickering
in his look, as through his voice the sirens
singing;
            that so tangy sprig which kept
a sorceress humble, loving, near as now,
sometimes swirling out within his breath
her wayward scent.

As starting up again,
the joyous grapple; and at once, snuffling,
beasts between them, the rank sweat, a marsh's
under-musk, soaking their pelts, behind it
ocean's biting souse.
                       Compare a Circe's
    airs, keyed to the silken score
    upon her loom and mingled out
    in cedar smoke, in smoky thyme,
    a fragrance binding every sense,
    with his wife's customary chores?

    Like one commanding a storm-
    struck ship—or ship becalmed,
    with a ragged, mutinous crew
    its storms, stuck on this rocky
    isle, the madly blooming things
    threatening to run amok—
                            plenty
    here for her to lift voice to,
    but hardly such in silken, soothing
    harmonies.
                  Yet had she, like that
    charmer after all, not changed
    the suitors—bound by few things
    only, their designs on her,
    ambitious to devour his estate—
    into fat, rooting pigs, geese fat
    for slaughter?
                     Forgive that Circe.
Forgive also—grateful to—those nymphs
and goddesses, the women whose great love,
collaborating, helped to keep him, keep
him, hale, for her.
                     Recesses they were
where he recovered in. And most of all

‹ 191 ›

as he, emerging headfirst, feature for feature—
his eye seeking hers, seeking him—
from out her hand, shies off her daytime doing.

XIV

For suffering the bitter weather of his wars,
the battering sea, how different he must look,
how like a stranger.
                    Why any tattered beggar
might be he. That straggly greybeard, say,
rags bunched on a stick, and many a day
skulked about their grounds.
                            Her gaze
fixed on far distance, on an image graved
into her memory, can she take in
this lout by her, the story he'd be telling?

(Any more than he the country he pines for.
No doubt he thinks he can shuck off,
and all at once like rags, the tangled past,
its spells and lulls in their enormous power.)

Fooled before by her unruly eagerness,
snatching at rumors, greeting every stranger,
time, sufficient time, her mind must have.
No lumbered, hollow horse for her, no midnight
storming of her gates.
                      Betray her lover, host
to every pleasure, for some beggar, shaking
hand held out, a filthy cloak clutched
round his body, no less foul, and old
enough to play her husband's father?—she
now old enough, lithe, lovely as his mother!

(Yet his travels heavy on him, blessings
of survival, rippled through his arms, how he,
grappling, felled that churl a score years younger.)

Twenty grating years to be so casually
cast aside? For has it not, that mountain
of time, by what they have put into it,
become almost insuperable, precious, hard
and hard, an iron?
      Treat it now mere summer
snow, a drifting mist! Or equally dismiss,
a movable, removable, like their bed,
her steadfastness.
     There, as in her dream,
she stands, never, though the world crash
down upon her, shifting, never yielding.

So much washed away, the rotted crops,
the vineyards slumped, the years nothing
but exploring, slow perfecting, of her grief,
now open herself to these appeals, expecting
a new zeal of her, fresh suffering,
another perilous life?

  XV

      Still he wooingly—
her name, brought home to her upon his lips,
new lit by its renown in all the world—
the gust of him, sprayed from the breakers,
would regale her:
      tale a kin to others
he has told, and like them subtly twined
with truths. For being pinned together
by the brooch she gave on parting, telling.

(Prickly now beneath his cloak,
a jabbing at the heart: the agony
of that hoof-flailing, golden deer,
a golden, snarling dog clamped,
solder, to its haunch.)
                              Tale glamorous
as he has been, the tunic, woven of love,
she wrapped around him leaving.
                                  Tight-fit,
shiny as an onionskin, to draw her
tears, he sparkling the more for them,
and that way draw her near like women—
droves of them, she gathers—gladly won.

But still she takes her time as he knows how
to do, for waiting's what they have together,
have apart, proved most accomplished in.
Both understand, like stars, tales of such deeds—
the lightning and its thunder laggarding—
require time, time to be heard, be felt.

Had they not learned it at the first
from one another, earth's own seasoned dance,
the measured pace of things completing
themselves,
                    from their dear time together,
the great tide washing over them, yet lovely-
slow, as honey, pouring from a vase?

XVI

Time ripening for the bow, she, lingered
in the dim light, is about to bring it
from the storeroom, hands still warm on it,
with hers his, summoning its past while relishing
the pleasure it will soon, become a swallow-

twangling lyre, loose.
                    And revolving it
for wear, worm-borings, while he's been away,
the glamorous stranger, always expected,
all ways surprising, dawn arising headlong
for its travail with the sea.
                    Now gathered—
plummet-time approaching—like that bow,
its long starved arrows, through her skein
that sped them even as it held them back,
the room about to burst, a fired rush,
one ricochet,
                    but slowly, slowly . . .

As You Like It

An old master yourself now, Auden,
like that much admired Cavafy and those
older still, in this you were wrong.
                    People
are not indifferent, let alone oblivious,
to the momentary, great scene.
                    No,
like Mrs. Gudgeon, the smart little char
come with our London flat,
                    listening
to the wireless, a most impressive array
of "the best minds"
                    engaged in difficult,
arduous talk, and she intent on it,
to her husband's
                    "What're you listening for?

You don't understand a word they say,"
rejoining,
        "O I enjoy it, just the sound
of it, so musical. And anyway I take
from it whatever I like,
            then make of it,
in my own mind, whatever I will,"
like Mrs. Gudgeon
          most of us, watching
the moment, some spectacular event,
be it Icarus falling,
          Cleopatra consorting
with the streets, or the astronauts
cavorting on the moon,
          bear off those bits
that we can use. This is the greatness
of each creature,
        the mouse at the Feast
of the Gods, one crumb doing for it
what heaped-up platters cannot do for Them.

Views & Spectacles

It's Greek glasses I want,
that's just what I want,
to see Athens, Ithaca, Parnassus
undaunted by the centuries

the Vandals overran, the Romans
and the Turks, the loving, paint-
removing, professorial Germans,
and in every firefly

                    a spark
that's Troy before, during, after.
And, to be fair, a Persian pair:
if I'm to see
          what's here
as well as what's been there,
why not—the sea obeying Xerxes,
waves salaaming
                    like trees
which doff their leaves before
the winter's huzza, many horsed—
what might have been?
                              I also
want a pair that focuses French
so that every "cave" I enter
is my favorite haunt.
                    I'm tired
of those so haughty, volubly
gesturing words hissed out
like a snake,
          ruthlessly
outspoken before my very back,
rebuking my accent for its being
quite obscene.
          I'm tired
too of impressionism, its gloss
& flair for making the most
(that solid tide
                    in green,
in red, is it flowers, mountains,
heaving haunch?) of what's a
casual least:
          why must
every flyspeck in each field
be designated flocks, haystacks,
crows to make it real?

‹ 197 ›

                    And why,
Nana bending, should we have
to see the stains detailed,
alfalfa, clover?
                    But I want
a pair—that's why I have two
eyes; though I'm myopic, I'm not
a dunce Cyclopic,
                    roaring
epithets irrelevant—which spots
at least two times at once
or routs
          the blur & tense
between what's in, what's out;
too often fallen between, I speak
in vain.
          Glasses, reflect!
Be Sanskrit, Eskimo, be ultra-
plain. The latter's surely nearer
bears & snow
               than anything
I know; the former's now engraved
into the open face, the first,
of dawn.
          But finally I must
admit that most of all I want
glasses which, quicker than fists,
eliminate glasses.
                    Certainly not
my nose squashed everlastingly
against the candy windows
of the world
               but of Olympus
a bifocusing, or simply something
godly: to wit, at once to see
and, seeing, be.

‹ 198 ›

Things of the Past

"Your great-grandfather was . . ."

And Mrs. C, our tart old Scots
landlady, with her stomping legs,
four bristles sprouted from her chin-
wart, she who briskly
                      chats away
about Montrose, founder of her clan,
as though she's just now fresh
from tea with him,
                    regards you
incredulously, a bastard gargoyle
off some bastard architecture,
one grown topsy-turvy:
                      "Not to know
your great-grandfather! How do
you live? O you Americans!"
                          She
cannot see what freedom it affords,
your ignorance,
                a space swept
clear of all the clutter of lives
lived.
        And yet who can dismiss
her words entirely? It burdens too,
this emptiness,
                pervasive presence
not a room away that, no matter
how you hammer at its wall,
refuses to admit you.
                As though
you woke and in a place you thought
familiar,

then had a sense (what
is it that has been disturbed?)
of one you never met
                yet somehow
knew—looks echoing among the dusty
pictures:
          that myopic glass
reflecting, like a sunset lingered
inside trees,
           a meditative smile:
a breath warm to your cheek,
your brow:
          the hand (whose?)
moving on your blanket in a gesture
that you fail to recognize

yet know it as you know
the taste through oranges of sun-
light current in them still—

then gone as you began to stir.
And for a moment dawn seems lost
as in a mist, seems wistful

for a feeling it cannot
achieve . . . the sun breaks through,
an instant medleying the leaves.

A Charm Against the Toothache

By these windows we perch, tourists
still, in a cuckoo clock, this starred,
three-storied hotel.

                    The cabinets here,
filled with random, little things,
porcelain shards, contorted figures,
seem to be exhibiting leftovers
from a flood,
                    like the hotel teetering
on a cliff, its rocks at tumbling,
breakers in recoil,
                            a halfway house.

Up against it wide open space,
with meadows far below—herds grazing—
gracing the panes, we urchin cherubs,
backs turned to the church-capped heights.

Behind us also, just beyond the road,
the town itself, sprawled uphill
that the sky looks as if it's spilling
over.
            Is the whole town asleep,
napping in its shade-drawn dark?
Or did its people wander off
with the army that once encamped
among the valley's slopes and meadows,
in their fashion tourist too, waiting
for crusades to sweep them off?

Or like us are they sightseeing
in Copenhagen, in Schenectady,
wondering what those stuck in Vézelay
are up to?
            At least oil-trucks
clatter round the bend; brakes jam,
screeching like a cargo of wild animals.
How it flails, that fox tail
from the latest lumbering down.

‹ 201 ›

While the light's still strong enough,
let's start the famous climb.
Famous once, I tell my students,
highway to a star-roofed city;
not as now a dead end to the past
abandoned.
        No doubt the villagers,
backs aching as they toted the church
up rock by rock, had reason to adore it.

Restlessness at them, ache
of a tooth that never stops, maybe
for a time at least they shed it
in the churchyard at the top.

What a tourist jumble, this path,
of shops, mouse-holes in the walls,
showing off exotic stuffs—
exotic in Vézelay!—
Indian bags, Parisian skirts
that I'd look Aztec in, and hempen
baskets, belts, from Jerusalem.

No doubt what the earlier pilgrims
must have put up with. Trinkets,
snacks and drinks, phony relics,
clay-baked monkey saints, martyr-
looking truly!
        Bring one back,
puff over it hard as I might,
my students would never see the flame,
only the gritty, crumbling dust.

For the houses crouched along
both sides, gates barred, windows dark,

forbidding backs, I feel no farther
off from home than home itself.

What's home in a world flits by?
Like trying to nestle on a storm-
tossed sea. And we, each one a medley
of cells, atoms in a maelstrom,
performing their St. Vitus dance!

Ah that enviable wife of Bath,
ever more at home the madder
the jig. On permanent pilgrimage,
her body the welcoming Lady Chapel.

No less the Faithful Ones, believing
with their sheep that the grass
beyond their reach was evergreen.
Restlessness—not destination—
also their resented, chosen lot.

But most I envy those in Schenectady
who care to be living nowhere else,
the local Woolworth's gewgaws
their true relics, movie houses,
banks, and bars their heavenly hangouts.

Well, we make do with what we have.

Though we moved from town to town,
my hands recall cracked banisters,
in rain wool smells like snuffling
animals, and I at a mirror, frozen,
drowned in my own pimply stare.
My ragged doll alone gave back
the love that I poured into her.

Beside my sister, twin yet pretty,
out of ribbons palely shining,
I a feather swirling from the wing
of some wild-flying, ice-&-wind-swept,
never-minding thing.
      And still
those thickets, snarled by vines,
my memories, scratching, clutch at me.

My suety aunts, forever fussing,
pinching me "Sit still!", gabbling,
nibbling, one fatter than the next,
their armchairs squat, stuffed like them,
smelling of mold, I, like our zoo-
crammed tigers, pacing inside a roar.

My parents, also keeping me leashed,
spent their care upon my sister.
It's true, I did rail at her.
How could I watch her disappear
into such stony, yet anguished sleep?

At last they packed me off to school,
a dismal jail. Yet happier
than facing them, mother's chatter,
her ratty neckpiece of a fox,
its beady eye hard fixed on me.
Fox in the attic, fox in the closet,
under my bed, glared from my dreams.
Or father's ever looking away,
eyes pale with miles of empty sky.

Again and again I'd hop a bus
just to be moving, going somewhere.
Safe only while we rolled along,

rain tapping at the pane, or snow,
ghost eyes peering, recognizing.

Dawn, rising, made a rose-
flamed window: sunset: starlight.
Highway we call it; high way it was—
our Notre Dame—to heaven.
                    Meantime,
two by two the passengers slumped;
pews they filled, carved-out figures,
yet flying with me in a private,
feathered revery.
                    And there,
still at last, still in the eye
of the storm, blissfully alone.

Like being transported through twilight . . .
our secondhand Apperson, fancied up
with cutglass vases, ruffled curtains
swaying, zooms along, father driving,
as if straight into a lucid dream.

Clover incense-like wafts round,
honeysuckle, lilac, twining
with the grown-up murmurs. Wheels,
the engine, tuned in on the spheres.

Yet even there in dreams father
stops the car (has the gas run out?),
shoves the door: "You're on your own."

And where, the years sped by, faces,
buildings, cities, flicked away
faster than an eyelid's blink,
am I?

　　　　Still fragments of my first
small town remain, its homespun people
fixed like hacked out, graveyard
statues.
　　　　　A smoke drifting off,
I take myself from clouds and brooks,
from every leaf waving farewell.

Like that day on a road somewhere,
a drizzle, with nothing to do
but walk on and on. Never a body
except maybe some bird going
its own way in the darkening sky.
Nobody knew where I was, I not knowing,
the land casual, lopping, as though
absentmindedly dropped, a lazy
man's curved whittlings.
　　　　　　　　　Till I came
to a barn, the piled hay smelling sweet,
and no one there to fuss or chatter.

I asked to sleep in it.
　　　　　　　Next morning,
waiting at the door, bread and coffee.
A place complete it was. But had,
alas, no longer than passing through.

And circling still, as though hoping
to find that place again, I babble
like the natives, no doubt prompted
by this spot and by that millrace
far below, the women working
near it in the field, like poppies
bobbing under the church's frown,
shadow once countrywide.
　　　　　　　　　But now

‹ 206 ›

no longer menacing, its portals
yield to our touch.
                              Grey light.
Damp, moldy smell. The stone-cold floor.

Look up. See the figures squat,
foursquare on the church's capitals.
Caught they are, fixed by nightmare
faces in some ancient pagan rite.
While doubtless down below the pilgrims,
too poor, too numerous for lodgings,
slept huddled on the stone-cold floor.

High over them and, as at first,
leading the parade, glaring though she
is, and runty, Eve it must be,
root-gnarled with the trees
writhing round her and her mate.

Stark naked like the rock
she issues from, she offers him
an apple rounder than her breast.
Passport to the world?
                              At core
the worm curls up, knowledge
pitted enough to break the heart.
Their hands touching as they try,
she and he, to cup that apple,
keep it intact from their fear.

After them that must be Noah,
set on a breaker-wrinkled peak,
topping this peak, the Ark by,
a wicker, big, one-windowed basket,
Mrs. Noah looking, bug-eyed, out,
tugged between the yet to come,

‹ 207 ›

the yet to go, the animals,
a ceaseless rustling, just out of sight.

A rustling—the lion loomed above,
and, after it, two elephants,
the pelicans their sculptors never saw—
menageries galore traipsing along
the margins of illuminated texts,
from out of fantasies, nightmares.

A rustling over me! No dream
it was, no fantasy. A body
striding, stalking, something out
of farfetched scenes, he Adam
to my Eve, expecting me to be forever
caged, caged like those couples
handcuffed to their capitals.

Like them I also kept an ark,
crammed with fidgety creatures.
Whatever course I tried to hold,
the voices raucous, bodies jostled.
But at times they chirped a song.

Not like those animals, packed day
on day in one small, stinking box,
ravenous enough to eat each other.

Land once more appeared.
This pile of stones, much stonier
than its builders meant, call it
our Ararat?
       A Rock of Ages
once, sheer eloquence of prophets
towering spilled over it like summer
rain.

Then hatreds gutted it,
rebellions, envy, pride. Next it
was sold and finally restored,
a monument, a tomb, the spirit flown.

The waters receding, dryness settled
in, dust on dust, what sorry beast
loves snuffling round such husk?
And shall these stones cry out again?

Yet the figures in very homeliness,
with their carvers lost inside the work,
believed their moment monumental.

Static though they are, they move
beside us, granite in our speed
and broken off, forever apart,
parents,
   sister,
     husband,
       aunts,
and I,
   stuck in our more than rock-
carved pews.
     Yes, like this place
haunted those figures' originals were
by every antic image as it scoffs
away: mischief, folly, envy,
lust, the passions in their jeers
gorgons petrifying themselves.

Us too as we gape up at them.

Tail end of their procession,
must we be bearing their wedged rock
that they look back at us?

                              Who's
to say we're not what they have come
to, their lone heaven? One dusk, one cold,
we share with them, one stoniness.

Pretense of standing still!
                              Writhing
stone we are, writhing like them.

So this place is little different
from that grey Schenectady.
Oil slick on both waters, fish
die in crowded shoals. Birds plummet
from their skies; for mercury rots
the air that song once cleared,
sparkling of seraphim as they
repelled the devils. Or so men then
read those heavenly commotions,
savage enough to scourge the earth
and all in it. As we are ready
once again to destroy ourselves.

The beasts in us, arked in sea-
sick feelings, trumpet out the rancors
stifling the hard-pitched body.

No wonder restlessness,
an ache, is all the rage: a fox's tooth,
the snake's, and mother's rampaging.

Still one reassuring thing
I stumbled on from out the Middle Ages,
a charm against the toothache:

        "Walk thrice about the churchyard
            and think not on a foxtail."

Should we try it now, circling
that weed-clogged plot, its graves
on graves many times forsaken?

Rather lean on this low wall,
extremity of Vézelay, vast supervising
of the gradual hills, azured
with distance, the vineyards, the winding
roads that, entered, seem to linger
in mist-shaded patches of the woodland,
alive with swarm after swarm of night-
ingales.
        Even with the trail slimed
over like a slug's, clouds of pollution
left behind by trucks, it's clear
why I prefer that bus, my travels.

The feral smell of gasoline
I've always loved; spilt on earth,
one vibrant stained-glass window
it becomes.
        Ground in its atoms,
fossils racing, bison, reindeer,
as along the rock of hunters crouching
in their smoke-filled caves.
        After
countless aeons the animals plunging
still, as I rush on in plane
and bus.
        This height speed and travel
enough for you? It does command,
this low wall, the summer's rambling
countryside, we everywhere
at once.
        But look! Down there, a couple
picnicking, what's that tugging

‹ 211 ›

at its leash?
          Looks like a bobcat,
a furry cub? Oh no, it's a white fox
flicking its tail!

The Cure

And what can you appeal to
if you have nothing but this language
to handle your feelings, this rout
altogether Scythian, say?
                    If blares
blow up in you drowning out each tootle,
simultaneously you their puny pipe,
your flesh the jettings?
                    You watch,
cowed by your body's brute enchantment,
truths, chimerae, rousing. Sinking
in this flood of voices,
                    English,
you think, to accommodate such tidings!
But its deficiencies become speech
also, silences a grace,
                    chinks
which let the antediluvian dialects
resound; epochs too—tribes of dialects—
not yet.
          And you are abounding
in the middle of a medley flouting,
by its bedlam, time itself: an only cure
for the vivid bane, the sometime

curse, of clarity. Nothing
but this English, tatters flapped
around the giant-bodied blast, streamers
that applaud the rapture passing.

See, it sweeps everything
before, mobs speechless, capsized
in this turmoil, satisfied that no voice
lives can sever it from itself.

But then it is, like rain,
a vernacular which nothing can translate
because it refuses to relate, its own
nature all that it relates.

The Library Revisited

"Weiss," a new anthology observes,
"is even able to be quite cheerful
about the burning of the library
at Alexandria."
              A scholarly book
relates that ages long predating Rome
and Alexandria, exemplary though they be,
already had remarked
                    the artist's
predicament: competing with the awesome
past. Thus I am positive the latest
of the great
              Cro-Magnon masters,
pondering the Michelangelo among his

‹ 213 ›

predecessors, as he beat his matted brow,
his wooly chest,
          had all he could do
not to haul up his massive boulder club
and finish off that handiwork. O
there they sped,
          the birds and beasts,
forever grandly caught, and only lesser
ones remaining for his careful daubs
to trap.
          According to that book,
in the Eighteenth Century "the thought
was to cross more than one mind
that the burning
          of the Alexandrian
library had its advantages." What would
those minds have said to the clogged-
up libraries today?
          That modern
English anthology alone, accounting
for a hundred years, sports "over 1200
poems by 155 poets."
          In the middle
of our florid fall, blinding in its sun-
beat spell, shall we try saving all
the lovely leaves
          and all the seasoned
tunes these birds, departing, spill?

The Late Train

What's it like?

A horn suddenly jammed
in a car junked years
ago.
    An alarm
gone off in a town
that a volcano leveled.

Or, snarling out
in me, a siren that must
belong to a time, a far-
off country
        I have
never known, shrieking
like a jet-black van
lurching
        to the wrecks
it's most successful in:
my countless relatives
minus
      faces, names,
mumbling from flowers,
birds, this windy smoke
clotting up our sky.

Throttled before
they got their word out,
it must break through
some way.
      How satisfy
except to let it go
and listen

                till it runs
its course, father,
mother,
                else a curse
choking itself, choking
him it's locked up in.

Before the Night

One poet tells us
of blinded children beating
at their eyes, perhaps to strike
the sparks from them of light
burnt out.
                And another
is much moved to make a poem
out of a report that H. D.,
having a stroke, fiercely desires
to communicate
                and "strikes her
breast in passionate frustration
when there is no word at her
tongue's tip."
                No word,
no word wherein before one's
heart was gratified, a jetting
out as of a fountain, fire,
lute.
                No word, no sight:
one beats against the wall,
be it blindness, be it flesh,
the body

‹ 216 ›

                    turned to stone
against the wish that Lazarus-
like would rise.
                    As she, a lovely
poet once, now, at the end
of sight, those children
at the start, haunted by all
the light
                    that they were cheated
of, beating, beating, bird-like
thrashing, in their own bones
prisoner.
                    A fired, stony gleam
for us who still can see and see
the blinded priestess, writhing,
racked, on her enormous sight.

The Polish Question
for M. L. Rosenthal

I

Suppose your powers such
you finished every poem painter-wise,
the light, its bias, so enduringly
sealed in—regardless of the time
and place the reader pondered it—
exactly as you wanted it to be
on this particular line, on that.

Suppose you gave instructions
at the relevant moment: "Pause here

to drink a glass of icy water so
that in you winter know itself,
you know yourself in winter."

"Honor this empty space (

)

as the place where what can not be
said, of course the most significant,
is being accorded a total hearing."

Finally "At the dots (. . .) the reader
is expected to think of his beloved
in her most memorable stance,
one so compelling it inspires
fear at storms already storing up,
her radiance, for drove-rich shades
attendant on her, troubling the more."

For is not Poland, Poland
of your grandparents, of terrible
times thereafter, waiting everywhere?

   II

By this eye, north of its frowning,
Poland lurks;
                    inside this finger,
sheathing its arrows, in itself
so sensitive to, so lusty of,
the slightest pain,
                    yet also
sheathing silks of a tenderness
that quickly knot—sleight of hand—
into a lash, a noose, a shroud,
Poland, Poland,
                where the sleeping

cat curls up, a scratchy, burning
bush, the porcelain cup a smashing,
through the cracks of which storm
troopers pour, as through the mouth
most cooing musics curse.

                That light,
and by this eye, should light, so
buoyantly, impartially, on such
a gross array.

            As though the sun,
nestled in dung, sees prodigalities
it can perform.

III

           A painting, finished
in the light of Normandy, is bound
to differ from another done
in Burgundy.

           But a Normandy work,
carted off to Burgundy, how would it
look?

        Try pondering it in Africa.
Siberia. Or a country which unites
those two. You did say Poland's
waiting everywhere?

            A Polish winter
lit—each flake a wick that focuses
ice-hearted hell—by tallowed rags
of flesh, by crackling, bloody cries.

And can we, so set off, warm hands,
warm hearts, at this and this and this
artwork for what each one supplies
in its fragility of paradise?

THE THEORY OF REPETITION

Well, is it not the virtue of art
that it, somehow surviving, happens again
and again?
      So the shot in the cinema
of the exploding tyrant's house which goes
up in elegant, slow, silky-colored smoke
a dozen times.
       As Hector over and over
and over—their chase as well, like racing
round and round a vase—
         is had by Achilles,
who would have killed him if he could
a hundred hundred times, but only
in the *Iliad*.
      Each time however
differently if only by the repetition
of the explosions, fatal draggings, gone
before.
      Or thirteen ways of looking—
one's remarking it a second later, thoughts,
new light, and other events intervening—
at a blackbird.
      (Similarly a coward
dies a thousand deaths, yet so perhaps—
unlike the low-nerved, brave man—
lives a thousand lives.)
       In other words,
as Heraclitus said, You cannot, even
at the seemingly identical place, step
into the same
      movie, love affair,
despair, joy, composition twice.

IV

Stacks of illustrations
           (paintings
piled on paintings here, like leaves
from under maple boughs, all mixed
with apple, sycamore),
              collected
out of Burgundy as out of Normandy,
reflecting on each other,
              lamps
with tawny, skin-taut shades ajar
to ponder them,
          the generations
falling leaves,
a rubbish their pale bodies
raked, anonymous far as the eye
can see, the teeth amassed, shining
in one steady grin,
          a gilt that,
striking, reinforces heaven's gaze.

V

Thick smoke coils up, the shriveled
leaves, the shoveled lives, the sky
one darkening cloud.
          Back those eyes,
those lidless, bloodshot eyes,
into the light.
        In sleep, in wake
your body, like an earth, is quaking,
like the waters, choked with cries . . .

VI

O, no, except for newsreels, books,
dispatches, most of all from dreams,
and the daily anguish of my mother,
ashes wind-strewn nearly twenty years,
I've never been to Poland.
But often
now I shudder at what the morning
light is likely to reveal.
Then Emerson
in his benignity chimes in, proposing
we accept "our actual companions
and circumstances, however humble
or odious, as the mystic officials
to whom the universe has delegated
its whole pleasure for us."
At once,
mid-sauntering up his slippery mountain
to the Castle, a later, dapper, Chaplin-
esque explorer of our circumstances
and companions, officials scarcely humble
but to perfection odious, leaps to mind.

VII

Over the phone a good friend asks,
"You know the latest Polish joke?"

Watergate its crux, the next
the hottest thing in transplants.

VIII

Words, words, such deeds words, come
from Poland or America, can do. (Words,

‹ 222 ›

so to speak, felled Jericho.)
                    Another friend
from London, hearing an earlier version
of this poem, says:
                    "The one thing I know
about Poland is that I'm responsible
for its bluebells.
                    A young translator
called on me and, much admiring my garden,
carried off some shoots,
                    then months later
wrote: 'Do come. Now Dannie Abse bluebells,
and several Dannie Abse poems as well,
are flourishing like natives in Poland.'"

    IX

We talked the last of the mild,
rain-grey Christmas afternoon away,
our old-world-courtly host, historian
of science, his vivacious spouse,
the political economist and his wife
in literature, pale for her trials
with remedial English, my wife's
musician brother, she and I.
                    Discussed
world politics, the desperate plight
of Israel, proposed some of the few
impractical solutions to that as to
the oil question—the Jews, our host
suggested, may have been at their best
diffused—
                    till the economist,
picking up his glass that brimmed
the day's dwindling light, remarked
in a kind of toast, like wine cast

‹ 223 ›

out across the troubled, oil-slick
waters:
>"Our views are all so grim
this may be the only solution."

Meantime, over the fireplace,
in deference to the painting's glimmer
never lit, the Monet meticulously
observed its delicate changes.

And as the party ended, standing
by the painting, our host, the woman
in English, and I, admiring the infinite
regression its pale, overarching
lavender suggested, a luminous fog
encompassing London Bridge, our host
said, "Yes, it repays study. Sometimes
I can see, far out on the horizon,
vistas usually shrouded."
>"What a thing
it is," I said, "this multiple vision,
this never-ending solution. I wonder
if Monet took into account—he must
have—the painting's future when,
as now, this scene, fixing an April
afternoon of 1903, submits to our looks,
the amber wine, the glancings, rainy-
mild, of Christmas, 1974."

x

>But suppose
you could, like a painter, nail down,
yet softly with the pointed brush,
your mood's each nuance—
>"emerald

green": "Pozzuoli red," splattered
like blood against a white backdrop:
and "raw sienna" (or is it "burnt"?):

"Italian earth," that "Naples"
like a lava, though the rapture
be Jurassic rather, Scandinavian,
a racing through the misty meadows,
but meticulously observed and fixed,
a cinematographic shot. What would it
come to?
   Nail it down and nail—
lid stripped away—the eye itself.

Enlarged then till its curdy white
became a screen, design with bloody
slashes like barbed wires marking
the juncture of the thing seen
with the feeling—transfixed
feeling—it released.
    Ah, will they
ever know what earthquake strokes
you undertook as the tremors began,
a hue and cry, Scandinavian, Polish,
rippling under your hand?
     Breathless,
you flung yourself out of the room.

ENVOY

So, to complete the spectrum,
for the last time instruct the reader:
"Wherever you chance to be, introduce
(and also, whenever, on rereading,
you may feel inclined to interject it
in this poem) a section of your own:

‹ 225 ›

a variation on what the rest
suggests to you or, if you prefer,
a departure, far as its antithesis,
an inspired or deliberate misreading,
a precisest disregarding.
                    And name it
after the room you are reading it in,
the room and time of its occasion,
you declaiming your spontaneous words
in the special dialect each place is,
letting them echo with—an underscoring
of—this purely local happening."

❖ ❖ ✦ ❖ ❖

FROM

Views & Spectacles

«1979»

❖ ❖ ✦ ❖ ❖

The Quarrel

So they hurried to the barn
which only they knew about,
for they had built it together,
the door where they wanted it.

And with never a hitch
they picked out a certain day
early in March, some thirty years
old, not moldier than when

they dropped it, a scrap
of churned-up cloud sticking fast.
They picked it because the day
they were in, hot, scratchy,

hulked there, dumb-eyed,
and they hungered for something
cold, biting even, garnished with
dangers. So, the table set,

they, finding their place,
gladly sat down to the feast
each time new, delicacies heaping
as they ate, more and more

strange guests, guffaws
like wine spattering the room,

the spot a steaming stew of odors
deepening all these years.

Sated, they slumped back.
And they were pleased to say
no more, already relishing dishes
no doubt simmering away.

The Rapture

You came in
and the rooms were empty,
all the breakfast dishes dumped
in the sink, scattered pieces
of bread, the butter melted.

And your heart leaped:
"It's here! The Time
has come. They've gone,
and I, I'm left behind!"

A cry clogged in your throat,
you rushed out of the house
down to the lower garden.
Maybe you could catch
a last glimpse of them
leaving.
       There, admiring—
arrayed in dawn, dew-waded—
early spring, the gnarled
crab apple over its head
in blossoming,

they stood,
their breath viburnum gusts,
caught in the current
of night, still drifting

downhill, its cooler air
mixed into the warmth
emanating from the earth,
stirred by worms and tubers,
groping their way:
                    everywhere
a gentleness, already
tinged by the promise—you,
your cry at last breaking
loose, heaved forth a sigh—
of brooding, savage summer.

Autobiographia Illiteraria

It's the lost, the hidden,
sections of my life, those pages
not yet come to, I keep
looking for.
            So I continue
probing, sniffing, like the cat
Hoppy whirled round and round
on the mat
            he's filled countless
times. And missing it in this
spot and that, a long trail
scored with ruts,
            I think

my missing means it's somewhere
there . . . like the woman who
collects dolls still.
               "Sometimes
I look at them, bangles, satin
sashes, mousy little shoes,
cluttering up the house.
               What
do I do? Rush out and buy a new
one. This Japanese with moveable
arms and legs,
           a swivel-neck;
the Hopi too—the Mud-Head Clown
askew—images Hopi children
can grow used to
            of divinities
who saunter down from the hills
to live with them a certain
portion of the year."
            Still
there is a side to the ubiquitous
familiars I've little inkling
of; still,
        beyond the smell
of myself, a strangeness which
goes out from me far as the world,
far at least as time.

Recoveries

«1982»

Recoveries

Day after day I work. For this I've come,
eager as some medieval pilgrim,
or that ancient wanderer, bent on the past,
the underground, to find his bearings,
worlds spanned, centuries.
                      This country's art
I learned from others, first from picture books
in black and white, in tints I thought—thought
till now—precise.
               And yet details of vantage,
which the naked eye must fail—unless
like mine it scale the painting—cameras,
deftly zooming in and out, command.
Pages, strewn about me, flurried so
I, flying, seemed to land upon one site,
another, of a church forever making.

Making here, as high on this scaffolding
I stand.
          The church's shady, tranquil cool,
rejecting summer, takes the traffic's drone
like mutterings of prayer. And yet I feel
the window-filtered morning as it angles
off these ancient stones.
                 Inching along,
light singles mica-flakes which keep the sun-
struck sky, reclining on the far-off peaks.
A certain crag composed these walls, still lofty

in its stones, still breathing out the snow-
pure air that cloud-banks once had pinnacled.
The church, battered by its years, remains
a heaven earthed.
                    And having reached this fresco,
morning startles at what greets it: embers
glowering, a tiger looms, a burning
bush; that redbreast, lit on its curved rush
of air, with each translucent, tiny bud
a ruddy daybreak.
                    Never see-through saints
from him who made the painting, never bodies
little more than twigs pale souls are perched
on to be taking off.
                    Whatever stains
accumulate, and cracks, time's handiwork,
God's plenty crowds the fresco still, a passion
for the praise that is exactitude.
And it exacts its niceties, as light
assumes each image easily as a coat
its maker first brushed, fitting—fit anew
for what the sun now does—on this disciple,
brine shone round him, on that brawny saint.

For what the sun and I, studying out
each hint, now do as we collaborate.

But caught upon the painting's jagged cracks,
the morning seems amazed to see the cross-
hatched lines of the sinopia peep through.
A sprite it looks, not yet confined, conformed,
by flesh's reservations.
                    Still the good
red earth that sketch is made of binds us all.

And binds me too, laboring to bring
to light again that pristine moment when,

‹ 236 ›

the master's last paints having barely dried
as now, my brush once more awaking them,
the early worshipers, who stood, stunned,
before the work, confused with what they saw,
for their time being completed it, this church,
its town, its noon completing them.

                        Their flock
contained those figures standing by to be,
in their red cloaks, accounted for; contained
that shepherd who, his body disappeared,
still blushes to the latest beams.

                          I too,
the sunlight in its freshness sealing them,
at last have learned by heart the fresco's every
shade and shimmer, each—the fresco, I—
the other's mirror, frame.

                    But sudden glare—
a stray mote bouncing off?—strikes—whose eye?
mine?

      A murmur grows, from out of figures
thronging the fresco's center focuses
into the raspings of a rusty voice.
Having turned, its owner, finger pointing,
pins me. Phrases splutter from his lips.

     I

     I speak that cannot speak, that have
     not uttered words—except to those
     few passionate to understand
     and able to—since paint lay wet
     along my mouth, sun fluttering
     upon the stroke as at my breath.

     Brushing my mouth moist again,
     assume that it must speak to you?
     Mirror, framed, indeed! You, squatting

‹ 237 ›

here, add touches that would be
an homage, blessing, to our fresco.

The years of all the centuries,
as dirt collects in sticky stuff,
mix in our paints (and never more
than with that recent mired flood)
till they've become one bulky coat,
its folds too packed to separate
(your skill intends to honor them?),
the guises, the disguises we
have had to don, as He did, pressed
into the dust-and-water mold
a mortal body is.
               And pressed
until he gushes forth one cry.

The air, the heavens, hardly large
enough to hold that voice's tidings,
they have flooded on. Still sound
through those can hear.

◇ ✦ ◇

                        Crowds earlier,
that, trooping in, had stopped by us,
would press us too. Instead their glances,
stuck fast, thickened time's patina.

You mean to wipe that all away?
Then how not wipe us out as well?

Ever now a swelling flock,
tricked out outlandishly enough
to win eyes more than my worn scene,

as if for some abandoned cause
it little knows, old comfort lost,
shuffles sheepishly round us.

Assured you know, tell me what they,
the generations upon generations
straggling by—our immortality!—
their fitful shadows squalling us
into a dun, expect of us.

But what can they expect who judge
us daubs upon a crumbling wall,
our red the usual hue, scant,
casual, as the things they are?

✧ ✦ ✧

Here I've lived. Lived, if you
would call it that, in contemplation
of the figure just beyond,
beyond him, where the fresco breaks,
the shepherd with a lamb slung round
his neck, all faded, flaked.
                              Yet shining
through them, as though interfusing
our whole sky, gaze of the One
the shepherd looks toward fixedly.

O yes, as you can see, He's gone,
gone except as something lingers
in the shepherd's look, in mine,
a kind of echoing.
                         And stationed
in the shadow, lasting—fiercer
than day's gleamings—of that One,

‹ 239 ›

I see.
　　　　For so I must. The vision
seeing is, intrinsic part
like tint indelible this fresco
cannot live without, has been
suffused through all of me.

✧ ◆ ✧

　　　　　　　　　　　　But who,
that other One apart, are we?

These, rigid, rapt in prayer, sharing
one look, like nimbuses their Christian
names attached to them, you can
identify: a frieze of saints.

Those too, heroic postures on them,
twined with great events.
　　　　　　　　　　And last,
drab as their order's habit, monks,
a parcel of our donors, slipped
into the fresco's bottom hem.
This they requested, hoping to be
hailed into some heavenly nook
where feasts forever wait on them.

I, standing in their midst, apart,
the visible I am, the seen
become the seeing, become the scene.
But someone not to be confined
to names, to local time and place.

All that had gone before, conjoining
with one moment's genius,

here crested out of paints. Those paints,
with fresco's self which must be swift,
by that moment's zest were fixed
into the singlehood of my being
wholly here.

◇ ◆ ◇

       Even so, new glances
stared at me, new guises I
assume, disguises.
          In my own eyes
by things they see, whatever image
shows, I must admit its truth.
Any surface, new light striking,
fancies shapes within itself,
gods and demons, never before
suspected.
         On such common mercy
I depend. Like a blind beggar,
his cup glinting in the sun,
here only when some money jingles
out the value stamped on it.

◇ ◆ ◇

I can look to myself as much
as to those slouching in the doorway,
bent on selling trinkets, pamphlets,
picture postcards of the church,
of us diminished and distorted.

Heat on them, as now, those hawkers
droop in sleep, a scraping breath

their thin lifeline.
                    The winter griping,
frozen, they become extensions
of the church's statuary.

Aping us, they liven only
when, their candles bought, a flame
is put to them.
                    The flame first breathed
in me ignites at likely looks?
Winds incessantly blowing have
looked after that!
                    An X I am,
marking this spot, scribbles on a wall.
Initials of a couple knotted
in a strange design which lingers
on though they've long gone, their names,
their meaning lost.
                    Lost not at all?
Rather I, prompting viewers
to a greater sense of self
and thereby to a deeper sense
of me, more and more am that
I am?
            Well, be it more or less,
since now your squinting nails you fast
to nothing but this wall, call me
the latest evidence of you,
the evidence such moment comes
to when one claims that he divines
another.

✧ ✦ ✧

Yet, joining the rest—
your strokings make it very clear—
you run my fellows here and me
together, even as you suppose
the underdrawing's red, my mantle's
hue, cloaks others wear, the flush
upon the shepherd's cheek and mine
the same.
          Deny it? See then what
you make of all the other reds:
that bud burst out into a rose,
that bird flaming across the sky,
the sky our window lets us see,
composing it, now roseate
its sunrise in the stained-glass panes.

All match those highlit splatterings
upon the Christ which prove a man
nailed to his cross can outsoar flight.

Soar most as, hovering like humming-
birds a nectar lures, five cherubs
cup His each drop's sacredness.
And cup through all eternity.

That moment supreme and many others,
different ingredients, a past
unique, have gone, forever gone,
into the forging of each red.

◇ ✦ ◇

Ponder it hard as you will,
you cannot track that color down,
its origin, the wealth it packs:

rows heaped on rows, ancestral kings,
all that they did and said, breathless,
just beneath the pigment's skin
waiting (at a touch from you,
a breath!) to blaze again wild days,
the nights, themselves a mine piled up,
smoldering.
                   Still you are right.
The red enclosing us, that rose,
bird, Man, and me, however fed,
whatever channels each may take,
such hues admit one lineage,
the good earth binding all.

                        ⋄ ✦ ⋄

Consider that fresco facing us.
Though it glimmers ghostly now,
departing's shade swept over it,
its several colors seem with ours
dipped from a single pot.
                            Yet senior
that the fresco is, its red
accommodating divers rust,
it looks on us as upstarts, friv-
olous intruders, here to strut
flamboyancy.
                   Its figures will
not, cannot, see—you notice how
they turn away—that we, a similar
vision pervading both of us,
regardless of our distinct miens,
endure one fate.
                      Resentment rather
that we've come to spy on them.

‹ 244 ›

They cannot understand ourselves,
like them, not more than prisoners,
one cold, one dark, our fellow world.

And rancor at our stealing looks
belong to them!

❖ ✦ ❖

              Despite their years,
despite the fading settled in,
their red like ours endures.
                    And were
there any look acute enough,
red's strokes, earthquaking still, reveal,
as if the earth should cleave, riches
in that painting as in ours:
ancient days like ingots, kings
in state, their radiance amassing.

Their old dauber, nameless now
as when his task took him by storm,
its lightnings for that moment his,
woke them, white-hot flakes shot forth
to make one heaven-flashing scene.

❖ ✦ ❖

Whatever greater skill he had,
so worked my master, swiftly sketching—
chaos first, its elements
aroused, embattled in his heart—
the world charcoal permits.
                   And then,
charcoal put by, red chalk assumed,

‹ 245 ›

his breath informs that chalk with lines
gone taut for humming out the thrashing
fish they've netted, precious catch,
foreshadowing us.
         As that old fresco
shows, so God employed the good
red earth that binds us all to fashion
men, His breath sealed in, like song
within a pipe, a clay-pinched, chirping
bird.

              ❖ ✦ ❖

    And yet wind, blowing, wind
that might belong to that first breath,
breaking through my master's breath,
makes knots or sweeps strokes hither, yon.
In fits and starts the work proceeds.

His chalk cannot assuage—its eyes,
still lidded, raking him—the tiger,
raging in its charcoal stripes.
Cannot assuage or shift, a burning's
black, that shrouded one—you see
him there, back turned and yet severe?

Sometimes the chalk runs wild, a squall
there is no banking.
         Then, his breath
a jagged cloud for churchly cold,
his face, his fingers something like
the hue he's made illustrious,
my master shakes as with an ague,
past what churchly cold can do.

Aspiring it is and dust
engaged, dust waging savage bouts
against itself.
        Some imp within
the chalk and him lays out—sly shapes
mounted on each stroke—a riot
of alike alluring courses.

✧ ✦ ✧

And more than that stood in the way.
Pored over us, a war of shadows,
monks, our donors, flail the air:
a blast, indeed the churchly cold,
would blow us out—too bold we were,
too live for them—into the dark.

Blow most, goaded by him, grimmest
among them with his cinder face—
be glad you cannot view it now!
He scowling-silent in his scorn
for all adorning save it be
the scant sort which the other wall
proposes.

✧ ✦ ✧

        Some deem his the form,
back turned, my master charcoaled in.
To never let him be, be seen.
And just, since he in his contempt
refused to countenance the earthly
world he made an irate part

‹ 247 ›

of.
    Others speculate the figure
is that One Whose look—the world
enhanced in its dear warmth—did He
turn round on us, must sear.
                        To you
both seem farfetched? And you suspect
none other than my master stares
into the scene?
               What he saw fit
to keep concealed I shall not now,
not even if I could, disclose.

❖ ✦ ❖

At last, unable to endure
the things which balk his vision, torn
between his own competing wishes,
claims his patrons would impose,
the price he has to pay,
               he rushes
off to leave us less than half
made up, a wisp of his bruised will
our own.

❖ ✦ ❖

       Returned (long he must
have stayed away: clad in their frowns
as in their black, many a time
the monks, wrangling here, stomped out),
uneasy truce,
          he scrubs away
those faces, limbs, his chalk too nicely

traced, hands, loose in the big wind
that blows through them.
                    Scene on scene
colliding—a fertility
outrageous sketching cannot keep
up with—the men and women, droves
of, tangled, founder in each other.
Destruction such creation's based
on, one body springing from another,
grinding and devouring as it springs.

Hard times also strike those he'd keep.
A tumult in us as in his blood.
Again and again he jabs at us,
no less the rubbing out, accused
that we, crabbed, proud, perverse,
conceal our virtues, spurn the shapes
we ought to be.

                    ◇ ✦ ◇

                    For all the flexing
of his arm, the furious strokes,
the furious strikings out, the strain
his thews and mind must undergo
against my will, my body's skilled
to try his craft beyond itself.

Locked in a grip he cannot break,
he stares at me. As you do now
for strokes I'd thwart.
                    Perplexity
plays on his face as if some shadow
of a deed too swift, too bright,
of powers much surpassing those

his earlier paintings had revealed,
teases his gaze. So tires him.

⋄ ✦ ⋄

Now, though he still leans toward me,
his eyes wander.
                    Distance in them
as a window frames the sky,
the houses, scattered by the hill,
the palace near, with lives in them
like fish in the river run beside.

Dropping the chalk, he hurries out.
And he is gone to what river-driven,
other life? The private time
he gladly spends elsewhere in one
such dwelling or another?

⋄ ✦ ⋄

                    Still
one day, long days gone by like night,
the dust heaped upon our chalk
which swipes have blurred, he dashes in.

A gleam surrounding him, a hum
of warm sounds pulses on his lips.
The monks, here too in knotted bunches,
grumble for the long delay.

But he, impervious to them
as fleas in buzzing self-pursuit,
us too, inside our chalk mere ghosts,
attends to some more taking sight.

⋄ ✦ ⋄

The monks in twos and threes creep out.
Assistants, summoned, carefully
prepare the scaffolding, the paints,
his brushes cleaned.
             The plasterers
prompt to apply the first day's coat,
at last the time for painting's come.

As he dips brush into the pot,
that brush then poised, a feathered thing,
his eyelids flutter:
                scenes he must
repeatedly sweep through, a bird
seeking its nest, the one secreted
in a shadow-littered wood.

The first stroke aimed, as it's put down
at once the forces of the world
converge.
            The fresco headlong, sure
against the hardening, its plaster
like a naked thirsting, sucks
each careful drop.

⋄ ✦ ⋄

              There my one eye,
glistening with the paint he plies
as with my first look's fluency,
a spark that sets all April going,
swifter than a bud to sunlight
opens!
        Watching, breathless I,
eye strains, unlidded, out to see—

‹ 251 ›

my straining helps and like a lamp,
casting light to see itself,
attracts—my other eye, the shape
my body comes to,
                    ramifying
from itself, an instant, blazing
tree luxuriant with leaves,
into my lasting pose.

⋄ ✦ ⋄

                    His hand
a new touch brims (informed with other
touches, blood-warmed, silken skin,
lingeringly musky?)
                    imparts a depth
of wonder, luster of a depth
of feeling, we could not know before.

⋄ ✦ ⋄

Yet that wonder he's brought back,
even as it spreads a glowing
like his gaze throughout my body,
rampant in the reds and yellows,
terre verte, burnt sienna,
rouses more in me, a jealousy,
swirled fire just beneath the skin.

Still I cannot long resist
this ardency which throbs through him,
his blandishments, his cunning hand,
deny the help that I must give,
that urgency which limns me in.

❖ ✦ ❖

Now eye to eye at last, he needing
eyes beyond his own, together
we peer at mastery required
that our eyes by hunger's strength
discover food, the food we are,
he and we each other's creature.

His rending rage as in the tiger,
jubilant with gratitude,
now turning powerfully tender,
smooths wrinkles out of him and me,
uncertainty's crude blemishes.

The day and night of the first day.

❖ ✦ ❖

First taste whetted, feast soon follows.
Next day's plaster spread, my master
speedily fills it:
                one taut stroke
the gist of tiger, paw explodes
to haul the panting body after;

swans, won of a single feather,
winged, full-fledged, from his brush,
out of their rufflings float a lake;

and rabbits, bunched, fuzzy smudges,
nibble in and out the edges
of the dew-and-shadow-dabbled
meadow.

‹ 253 ›

❖ ✦ ❖

Quicker than a foot
can climb, hillocks he mounts next:
a waterfall, in all its rushing,
upright, spouting still though paints
be crusted, flashing—sunlight spun
into its texture—like a temple;

by a grove which, rifted through
with nervous, blinking leaves and busy
little lives (those crinkles, are
they cricket cries? young lovers nestled
in their passion?), at the vanishing
point does not conceal the hoary
graveyard shaded by dwarf pines.

A look beyond, three towers, shot—
so fast his hand pursues its course—
like arrows greedy for their target:
stonework, sturdier than any
fortress.

❖ ✦ ❖

Meantime, to house
the rest, he rears high noon throughout
the fresco; massive building it is,
and yet a buoyant.
                    Banked round,
the noon is lit—as though that One's
regard still set—on leaves and rocks,
which spurt gold lava-like, on glances
spinning out, on cry-shaped mouths.

‹ 254 ›

Their words reverberate, a riddling
undertone, the way this moment's
sunbeams swim, within the paints,
schooled fish glistering their stream.

The senses wrung into one sense,
not only sight becomes a scene,
the greens and purples resonant,
but sounds and scents blow into hue.

Thought too and feeling bodied out,
the mystery of what men are
jets forth their fiery ambience.

❖ ✦ ❖

Jets through my master.
                     Even now,
whatever doubtings may oppress,
what dust the light is speckled by,
that primal breath abruptly starting
up again, the fresco twitching
like a beast, I feel him, warm
and knowing on us, luminous
his steadfast gaze, his hand still touching
through the paints, however settled,
vibrant in its span the world.

Once more we seem to be mid-making,
he, stroking us out, martyrs,
seraphs, pouring from the brush,
a torrent out of heaven.

❖ ✦ ❖

                    Out
of other spheres as well.
                    Earth blent
with heaven in his paints, his fire
fuses them.
                    Each stroke compiles
its cells in which an anchorite,
but coupled with his counterpart
in mortal combat, love immortal,
dwells.
            The many strokes combined
making a single, blowing field,
impassioned bodies loom, triumphant
and serene in very passion.
                        Living
creatures, no less lime, water
mixed with clay, no less than we
loom forth, a mystery.

                    ❖ ✦ ❖

So noontide lavish, plashed with him,
as though just stepped into his spot,
the shepherd stands, youthful, glowing.
Whole also, like the others, caught
within their stride, their ample garments
sails for wilful breezes gusting
through them.
                Action, even as
they bend into the quivering bow
of concentration, springs from one
blazed eye and hand raised to the next
around the fervent, central scene
though He's no longer part of it.

This incandescence that they kindle
by, fast catching like dry limbs,
my master takes his fire from
and feeds it, fueled, back to them.

❖ ✦ ❖

Although this fresco map-like keeps
the scorching route a tempest takes—
at moments some gust threatens still—
its fury blesses everything
it touches.
          But it plunders too
near countries, far, their crowded past,
to furbish us.
          At times no doubt,
hauling such spoils to his corner,
my master feels himself a miser, rogue.

And yet by fondling them he hopes
to make them his and more than his,
this nook become a center, see,
a port and haven of renown,
through which the riches of the world
must flow enhanced.
          The famous dead
wrung dry in us, his fellow rivals,
the most gifted tributary
with the serried kings and queens,
all help to swell his boldest news.

❖ ✦ ❖

‹ 257 ›

And when the light adjusts, as now,
the midday noon streamed in a light
yet certain leaning on our noon,
the hordes the fresco has consumed,
their glances, sparkle out a fire-
works befitting kings.
                            But no,
you cannot see—not in my eyes
their eyes, not all they'd done, the women,
flickering, they staked them on—
as in the making of a man,
the generations on generations
that merge to consummate this scene.

⋄ ✦ ⋄

And other imposing things there are
you cannot see: ships, cargo-crammed,
sunk to the painting's floor, its waves
closed over in a glossy sleep.

Till slowly rising to the surface,
answering this sunlit probing,
but suffused throughout the fresco's
flesh, thus visible and not,
crushed lapis lazuli with ocher,
umber, smalt, viridian
and other oxides from exotic
realms.
            Ores' fusillading looks,
enveined with secret reveries,
as high noon's tropic closes in,
expose their figures.
                            More than nuggets,
more than ancient, hardened days,

those kingly ingots, they explode
god-like from our master's dreaming.

With the day sodden outside,
a time for dreaming, for siesta,
it is that the noon be kept at bay.

✧ ✦ ✧

This day swiftly piled on days,
a cascade dashed down mountainsides,
far faster than the clay can dry
my master finishes.
               And finished,
paints and brushes, scaffolding
disposed of, he considers us
equipped, armed by his love, his craft,
to keep us here, outwitting worm
and wet, the worst that time can do.
An offspring on our own, we're left.

✧ ✦ ✧

While the town, sweltering, sleeps,
trace that far arch my master's built,
stroke fit to stroke.
              The arch admits,
softened by distance, bustlings from
the town beyond you almost hear
packed murmurs of as in a dream—

scarlet banners flapping wind
may token blood-raw war or fan-
fare of some gaudy carnival,

‹ 259 ›

the loaded, creaky wagon, driver
singing as he lurches, drunk,
or, shouting, lurches, drunk with rage,
to flog his mule—
                        confused with rumblings
and occasional cries, the town
adrowse where worlds ago dense arbors
danced around us, olive groves,
air laden with the scent of must.

⋄ ◆ ⋄

And now, lapped inside this coil
of paints, grown heavy in the late
noon light, the roses blotch; the bird
wings droop; wind, as though it's joined
the drowsing, nods, hunched up, dream-
less, like a locust in its husk.

Like the breath once rustled through
a pipe hung by the shepherd's side.
Then folded, puffy layer on layer,
breath sleeps within, till roused by sounds
suddenly recalled, the reaper song
it had swept up along with it.

That side and pipe long blown away,
you would blow them back again?

⋄ ◆ ⋄

The light grown silent, through this crack,
this, a fragment of the fresco
missing here, the underdrawing

shows, shows what, compared with what
we might have been, we have become.

Submissive to proprieties
belonging to our time, these paints,
drying as if by instant aging,
fit public faces on us all.

The wiry spirit we began
with, wild as in a wind, still beating
free beneath, the flesh conforms.
And we stand ready for display.

✧ ✦ ✧

The town awake, my master comes
with others. The garrulous flock of monks,
their purchase prized as if their hands
had fashioned it, gloats over rival
orders scowling.
                   Magistrates,
wool merchants, burghers, bankers, guilds-
men, suchlike worthies of the town
for whom my master's often painted,
bustle in to see themselves,
be seen, in church as in the fresco,
they, their world, immortalized.

Committed to a kindred work,
the making of the world in words,
his friend of the singed countenance
confronts us, multitude of one.
His gaze, whatever fire eats
at him, hammers sparks from us.

Our reputation spread, soon sweep
in lords and ladies, well attended.
Gems of them, their lustrous glances,
voices, mining out new gleams,
intensify the fresco's fame.

Our maker basks with us in praises
sung, the choir, joining us,
the masses of the town, in rounds
rejoicing.
       Till that fame hales in
far travelers. And for a time,
still new, the world around us new,
we also travel, colors, smells,
strewn over us, the jumbled sounds
from distant lands, and strange, that they
had wandered through, secreted by
their robes' stiff folds.

◇ ✦ ◇

          An early dusk
my master, much like you, slips in
alone. He falls into a study,
hushed that he seems one of us.

But then, brow wrinkling, he frowns
at what is happening, events
he has no inkling of.
         The shadows
shifting, sudden wit wrung out
from restless light and dark by chance
encounterings, it must appear
that we are bent on mocking him.

Once exposed, fame fancying,
we wear what looks men hang on us.
And time as well.

❖ ✦ ❖

Not only men.
One time, no one about, a figure,
hooded, slight inside its wrappings,
takes its station just below.

Instantly I feel that I
am looking up at her, but in
the lengthened shadows dimly seen.
Her garments fluted like a sculpture,
huge she seems, to the waist dark,
the face radiant.
Her gaze,
as though set off by what it sees,
now flashes fire. Beams of that
I felt when he first came from her?

Although beyond those probing eyes
we spy no farther part of her,
their gaze, having drunk its fill,
responsive to some thing in us
even our master failed, grows mild.
The glistening we bathe us in!

II

But that was ages, worlds ago.

The fresco done, my master gone,
new work proceeds. Here in this church,

‹ 263 ›

and yet beyond the church's rites,
the rites of passion swirl over us.

Amid the hush, night streaming in,
sometimes broken by light steps,
a sudden whisper, one or two
steal through, these with a squinny
looks about to scrape the coat
from off our bodies, pluck gems out
of diadems, gold-plated haloes!

Others also scurry by,
then stop in sudden weakness, fright,
bodies, breathless, strained toward us.

Or is it something else detains them?
Peer as I may, two faces moth-
like, beside a taper wavering,
how tell love from its contrary?

Scuffles, sighs maybe, a scream
cut off.
       The glints, are they reflections
from moist lips? A blade, blood-lit,
slashed across the fresco?
                See
that scratch next to your hand!

❖ ◆ ❖

                    At dusk
avengers come, their fury furled
round them religiously.

                    That fury
as they fumble in the dim light
spending itself, they disappear.

Though things I've seen cast certain shade—
rust splotches on my robe the sun
this moment polishes, they're nothing
but time's smudge? red only red—
those others, bent upon pursuit,
were too sunk in themselves to see.

Law, late, in purfled hood struts by;
so well encased, what eyes has it
for anything beyond itself?

                    ✧ ✦ ✧

Or now two gliding candles, paused,
light up the painting opposite
so that its figures seem to carry
on some secret rite.
                    The dream
their master served awake in them,
they strive to celebrate his saint-
liness, this way restore the mystery
his praying—hours rigid, self-
forgetting while he painted—made
him one with.
                    Like local actors
prinked out in their loose-fit sacks
(were they dabbed on, mulberry stains?),
cosily they live with reeking
goats and mules, the manger's glory,

shepherds gawking at the star,
whatever wrinkled babe it may
now have become.
Two strides from them,
we stand apart wide centuries.

❖ ✦ ❖

They proudly turn away, moving
hues we shall not see again,
their far-off era in its distance
on them with their vanishing.

Still out of them a certainty,
that truth, always more urgent,
always more lost.
Wrapped in tasks
they were created for, they do
not need to struggle with the knowledge
troubling us.

❖ ✦ ❖

Rarely now
the novices, each a green man,
trundle in whole summer, flowers
drowning us, sweet wilderness.

Rarely now the blare of trumpets,
buffeting our wall as though
to fell it, wakes the cornered angels
that the stones recall the music
so volcanic they like notes
had flurried round in till it massed
them.

‹ 266 ›

Blare confused with thick incense,
the church bursts open with a gay
commotion.
　　　　　　　Clad in robes like paints
newly splashed upon the air,
people march in slow procession.

Supervisors of the pomp,
we mingle with the lordly elders
and the bright-eyed boys and girls,
their warblings parti-colored ribbons
floating high the seraphim
delight to dress them in.
　　　　　　　　　But once
they leave we, like the flowers, may
fold up or like the banners, flung
aside.
　　　　So you might say we stand
uninterrupted down the years?
And stood save for the praises wafted
round?

❖ ✦ ❖

　　　　The praises that at first
rang out with equal fervor changed.
New preachers, passionate for doom
and rancorous, much like that cinder
monk, wind-howling some, a hail
of pebbles, pelted away at us
as at their flocks.
　　　　　　　These, wailing,
gnashed their teeth or, as though
to join our company, stood petrified.

$\diamond \; \blacklozenge \; \diamond$

To be flung, had we been portable,
with other follies, our poor fellows,
on the pyre.
          In the splendor
which our disappearing makes
at last immortal!
               Countless paintings
reprobated? Nymphs and satyrs,
yoked together, shamelessly
leap out their lust's extremity,
as in hell-flames their flesh's antics
helped to fuel?
            Others too:
artfully mixed, applied with care
my master would appreciate,
those paints precious to their users
more than prayers, than sacred images
they kiss, unless it be the image
close pressed in the full-length glass?

How should this not inspire blasts!

$\diamond \; \blacklozenge \; \diamond$

So, just below us, in a stormy
session, roused inquisitors
condemn—a litany the muttered
names, each lingered on to number—
diverse culprits, jumbled round
them on a table.
             Charges leveled
thunder so the veils which wind
and breath conspire to enliven

billow, silk, as though nude bodies
dance in them, quick to the light
of looks much like our colors.
                              Silks
and veils cling to those priestly fingers
even as they spurn; powders, plasters,
snaring wigs.
                    Next applications
for the ear, deft pipes, soft lutes.

Riggish the priests pronounce their tunes:
these, sowing themselves within the hearer's
dreams and wake, as promptly reap.

Let flames accommodate their music
to a last Magnificat.
So lofty music waits to be
released from what seems lowliest!

❖ ✦ ❖

And last, pored over them, as though
each were a casement onto hell,
those scrolls.
                    In their engrossment—faces
scorched a florid hue—nothing
other than religious zeal?

Dumped on the fire, Aretino,
till now cold for all his sighs,
is spouting heat and light at last.
And cries as well, cheek by jowl,
alas, with Petrarch and Vasari,
the painters' private lives on show,
Boccaccio and *Primavera,*

‹ 269 ›

scintillating as though gods
were strolling naked in its midst?

Such happenings I leave to you.
I see no more than looks reflect,
rumors crackling still with flames.

◇ ✦ ◇

The church, meantime, enacts the countless
scenes its paint and stone had figured
in.
     And still the battles roar
around us. Conquerors clanking through,
their armor's glitter clashes with
our gaze.
               There, just beneath our edge,
they meet to stake out rival claims.
But then, words rousing rage, the treaty,
its high-blown words still puffing air,
breaks off.
               One ruffian, kneeling
to receive the crown, another stabs
and, even as he stabs, snatches
up the prize.
               That despot and his kin,
securely guarded day and night,
the monks, their mass devoutly kept,
perform the deed a brigand dare not.
The cries add volume to the Dies
Irae.
     Silk, one patch, left fluttering
behind, ruddy as if dipped
in blood, appears ripped out of us.

‹ 270 ›

＊ ✦ ❖

Few notice this. The bulk, bent
on an assignation waiting, money,
plots, spend no more than a passing
glance on us.
    Except that one,
stumbled by his weapon, looking
up. And certain he reads laughter
in my face, half draws that sword,
but then, ashamed of his absurd
embarrassment, face ruddier
than ever, as he puffed in, puffs out.

＊ ✦ ❖

Such trippers flitter through. Enough
so that I can, times changed, keep time,
their costumes changed to say they are,
their gabble echoing those gone,
the same repainted.
    Burly some,
a troop, now clamber us with banners
rampant, rucksacks, hobnail boots.

But others blunder past, content
to undertake our lowliest foothills.
Eyes nailed to the back ahead,
each one the other's donkey-tail.
A flapping by, had they been wet,
would blot our paints.
    And do and do!
But mostly let the dust they stir
bestrew on us, the darkness darker

‹ 271 ›

for the dun-like, fitful dusk
their looking comes to.

⋄ ◆ ⋄

               Colors also,
shirt-green, -black, -brown, -red,
go marching through: men stiffer than we,
painted shadows, dreams, unreeling.

Someone, staggered in, a star
dangled from his arm, dragging
like a wing, falls at our feet.

The crimson, brimming from my robe,
clots his shaggy beard, his head,
slashed ruddy gold.

⋄ ◆ ⋄

           Now, dashing after,
anonymous as petty clerks
in greyish suits and hats and ties,
men circle him and, striking many
times—O could we spread our cloaks,
we, who have seen such deed over
and over, would cover him—they drag
him off. This silently except
for grunts and crackings which tell us
what bones are like, and tell, each gasp,
what life and death.
               The art's renewed
that put the seal upon man's hope
by way of one Man's doom. Incarnate
it must be each age.

Astonished by
that sight, one act uniting times,
we stand and, timeless, stand.

                ◇ ✦ ◇

Aeons
it may be, the dripping, is it,
from those wounds or from the moisture
oozed out of these stones?
                Aeons
or a day.
        Then suddenly like some-
one tapping up and down the roof,
a splattering begins. What light
there is blinks on, blinks off.
The tapping after turns into a roar
that says the sky has ripped wide open.

There, swooped on us as from wings
in waves, a flock of shadows capers
with the patriarchs,
                while blasts,
close-pressed, crescendoing—the dark
shot through by crowded torches—jolt
the church in every rock.
              The earth
it must be, cracking open, vomits
ingots, kings, their golden rage,
gay devils.
        Every martyr quaking
finally, the dove, its drove
of seraphs, moult. We also flake
away.
        Paints once more wet, our lake,

sprung from us and overflowing
its muddy banks, smacks of the sea
wallowing near.

❖ ◆ ❖

The welter soon
sets all afloat.
Soaked with others
in his streaky pane, pale his mosaic face,
Noah seems to weep:
"Not again!
The Ark, here dry-docked centuries,
must it endure another storm?"

Who would have dreamed the sleepy Arno
harbored the Flood!

❖ ◆ ❖

Eddying, the waters
ebb. And with them some of us.

As though abruptly summoned
by the truth that they had served,
a stool, a bowl, dropped in the rush,
our neighbors have drawn farther off
than ever.
Too late we realize
what gap they leave, our solitude's
chief company. And company
against the crowds.

❖ ◆ ❖

Despite the paints
discolored here and there, with gashes
one might think an imp's improvements,
dank restored to normal damp,
we take our wonted stance again.

But for that scabbed off, the stone-
like silence hemming, hard it is
to call back times we once had made
a lively part of.
                    Still the motes,
twirled in the light, rebounding off
the stone, resemble glimmers left
of angels,
            dreaming we drift in . . .

III

and each day dream a little more,
while they, this age's natives,
vibrations as of battering rams,
flock to the lure we are, a settle-
ment, so they would like to think,
against the madly swirling world.

See how they melt among the mob
that smites our Lord and, swelling it,
the mindless brawling, help fulfil
the whole, great, terrible story.
You too with every stroke you add.

These no less, still come to pray,
kissing away the feet of the stone-
twisted Christ that He must see
why He was crucified and crucified
again, the one successful portion

of His life. He hanging, nailed
there, as we hang.

❖ ✦ ❖

          Be sure no tiger
caged more tellingly, its raging
crammed within the tiny space
of repetitious, tail-twitched pacings.

You expect to climb these miles
on miles of nothing more than dried-
out, scaling paints which time becomes?
Bound as you are to your own present,
what past it can you know?

❖ ✦ ❖

          So now
you shiver for this dungeon air.
The church's shady, tranquil cool
a mountaintop indeed!
          This work,
first charged with crimsons like apocalypse
you strive to summon forth once more,
still dangles, a torn gonfalon
from some old war, in an abandoned
site of stone.
          So stony bare
these flocks dare not dawdle here.
How can we feed their basic hungers?

Still our lake, fish-scaled its waves,
yet racing too for shadows deep-
ening on it, looks as if it might
slake any thirst.
          As likely it
as bits of weed and scraggly grass-
blades, breaking through the crevices,
confused with fresco grass and weeds.

                  ❖ ◆ ❖

And yet it may be we remain,
like Lot's wife obstinate, a salt
lick for those few who, joining us,
look back.
          A salt lick and a light
like precious gems kept in a cave
that eyes might dazzle by.

                  ❖ ◆ ❖

                At first
our master and we were also rapt
by cavernous, rich light.
                But soon
the mind, so opened in this fresco
after animals, saints too, arose,
spewed trafficking, malicious imps,
exuberant to share their filth.
As if the radiance arose
to study out their churning void!

Then past those patriarchs and prophets,
things we clung to, stolid land-
marks, squat, opaque, benignly peasant.

Warmth they give off, glow, to succor
us, my master, me, still aching
at our loneliness your time
cannot suspect the fullness of,
the terror of that emptiness,
the mercy lost and from that One,
the overwhelming, tender power
that had seemed a touch away.

Glimpses of His love the shepherd
basked in, the departing sun-
set, in his crumbled cheek still flushed?
As at the common clay they share,
the common, irredeemable clay,
for which in His great pitying
He bore His final agony.

❖ ◆ ❖

Now long ages gone.
                    More gone
for what those ages ruthlessly
have done as though to underscore
the truth in His extreme torment,
the terror of our emptiness.

Not even His corpse sop enough,
the heritage those ages left,
the carrion, its ravenous
debris, grows hungrier consuming.

‹ 278 ›

Here, our strongest rites and customs
lost, the works you prize ghosts many
times over of long forgotten ghosts,
this church, a mortuary for
the heaped, devoured dead, hoards
emptiness on emptiness.

⋄ ✦ ⋄

Still some,
in quiet times slipped in alone,
as if the fresco, not yet done,
had just now, from a recess hidden
in it, loosed them, or as you
do lingering, again light us,
light we had forgot.
Luxuriating
in it, by your brush's strokes
(see how much you've learned from us!)
like wingings, we fly out as by
our master's strokings to those places
one time ours alone, the moment we
were meant for nearing.

⋄ ✦ ⋄

Now as near
as it can be? The heaven touch is,
stroke-sure, vibrant, as one meaning
twines a complex sentence?
Winds
can revel in a grapevine so,

‹ 279 ›

mining out of its complicated
tendrils a pervasive scent?

Such things I now can feel only
at second hand, a hand beyond
my maker's.
             Still this touching joins
us all, my master, saints and demons,
tourists too?

❖ ✦ ❖

             It may be so.
By what you are a few like you
highlight some section of the work
to find new bits of us, odd hues
not we, not nature, could have seen.

This one, gaze fixed upon my sleeve,
discovers daedal patterns there,
a landscape he then magnifies
to sprout a lunar scene's wild flora.

Or my garment's stains, for him
not blood, our dim, recorded past,
but mappings to the treasure that
lights up inside the mind alone.

❖ ✦ ❖

Time passed, some things, as if abiding
proper time, mature. The carmine
in that figure, standing by
the shepherd, mellows, petal-rose.

The fingers of his left hand bloom.
And springs to it—what seemed a blur—
a flowered branch, the lake reflecting
verdant shadows, strangers craning
just outside our scene.
     A shadow
such as yours upon us.
      Darkness
rushing in, last glisten, letting
go that branch slow leaf by leaf,
looks like my master's glance, the One,
a child's.
    Last glisten as this rose,
now closing, sheds a bit of color
on its neighbor while the redbreast
bundles in its wings as in a nest.

      ✧ ✦ ✧

But see what you have made of us,
changed from sacred things, a meeting
between men and God, to something
strange.
    Yet, stripped of everything
beyond our selves, that strangeness
can bestow a glamor still.
Shrines we remain.
      Your age's lust
for dusty shards and shells which echo
no Red Sea beyond your blood,
does it not smack of idolatry?

      ✧ ✦ ✧

Relics you're not after, but glimpses
caught in works like ours of the human
truth, the mind and senses' moments,
accommodating their kind of heaven?

Jacob's wrestle and the name
he won must mean no more to you
than our maker's struggle with his vision.

❖ ✦ ❖

And still the work we are remains,
a telling witness to that struggle,
like the angel hovered over us?

He, flown outside his parent heaven
near to earth, but winged so well,
from out his nimbus spins an Eden,
in this dark collecting.
                Winds
of where he once had risen, ruffling
in his feathers, flight that needs
no space and, yes, no motion, buoys
him still.
        Sufficient he as any
tousled thrush that dares to winter
in its trill, its courage spurred
on by the rugged marigold
its petals and its breath sustain,
as many florets in their self-
made neighborhood maintain each other.
Such warmth, though it be laid away
in ice and snow, by that is kept.

❖ ✦ ❖

People wandering past us,
for the local, daily things they use,
the bags they carry, clothes they wear,
that painted, frizzled hair, those shoes,
the landmarks of their time and place
uniquely theirs, look fabulous.

Even so they think them real.
                                   Just so
the world I am adheres to me
as to wet paint?
                        Leaves, how long
can they outlive the branch that bears
them? Carry, like an acorn stuffed,
a limitless fertility,
the past thirsting for its person
in the future, as though the future
already throbs, dependent,
to be perching on its limbs?

✧ ✦ ✧

So you, my future's present, strained
forward, reaching out, think you
obliterate the centuries
to touch beneath my robe a heart
still battering, its strokes pulsing
from my master's hand, his heart.

A splash of paint so radiant,
you are convinced, patches space
between the tiger and the lamb,
as it spans the gap between us both?

Unaware he'd draw you here,
my master, in a sense, paints you

in too, essential to the scene
(since now you have appeared): painting
goes on still.
        For eyes like yours
my hand, grasping this robe, hauls up
the beasts, my fellows, even far-
off, cloud-crowned hills.
             And you, by lines
drawn out of me, surprised, are hoisted
to a sky which dazzles you,
a sky dazzled by the gleaming
springs from you.

◇ ◆ ◇

         Times must be
themselves. Yet you believe that even
while they go their special ways,
times meet, and most of all in such
embodiments?
        So for the bodies
wearing us, bodies that you lend,
we shine forth, brand-new fresco?

But soon surprises that you find
in us worn off, we come to little
more than loot your mind has hung
upon its walls, framed images
mirroring you.
        There is a pleasure,
future, such misprising one
another prospers? Endless future
of a pleasure bound to grow!

For even while you ponder us
we, flattened back to peeling paint,
inside this darkness thickening
seal shut forever. Seal the more
for all the layers you apply.

✧ ✦ ✧

And so we linger on, not past,
not present, neither life nor death.

Even while I speak crumbling
gnaws away at me, a maw
incessant though it be unseen.

Weary of this rigid landscape,
the wind at last is shedding it.
Much like a music breaking out
of jail a pipe can be, it would
abound within the open sea
of air.

✧ ✦ ✧

          That air entices me,
the ceaseless murmuring which swift
wings, be it angels, be it gnats
in nation, make:
                    the murmuring
within the patch those teeming sun-
beams and wings gossamer spin out,
they wrapped in it (as our fresco

once kept us, we keeping it),
until, dissolving, they sweep off
with it.
     So I, like the shepherd,
always more strongly drawn to join
the One our eyes have never left,
the grip in all its rigor of
these paints at last cast off, I would
let go of gown and hill, you
and the rest, this will, now stiffened
into stone.
     I also would return
to mica-flakes before they flocked
into one beetling, hoary, star-
torched mountain which men ages later
carved into this crag-like church.

A wisdom I begin to know
beyond all wisdom, blessing, time's
scant joys: the radiance danced out
by nothingness.

◇ ◆ ◇

                    However much that dance
may satisfy, it soon must change:
the painting going on, the latest creature,
wave insurgent, leaf, bird, star,
supplants it.
     Thus, by being wholly fresh,
it saves—by making wholly new best serves—
the treasures else forgotten which belong
to you, your master, all who once have lived.

Its longing to be free most powerful,
the wind, escaped, must soon yield to some song,
whether it be man or tiger, painting
in between, to house itself, as briefly
you and I, paired here—your maker also
backing you—compose wind's latest scene.

And from now on, so let its moment bid,
each shade and shimmer of your fresco,
opaque, immortal moment of a red,
obliterating every argument,
every theory, doubt and terror, will
be flashing through my mind.
                              Now into night,
the precious mine of you amassing.

❖ ❖ ✦ ❖ ❖

FROM

A Slow Fuse

«1984»

❖ ❖ ✦ ❖ ❖

Camel in the Snow

Professionals of snow,
the Eskimos mint many terms off it:
snow-at-sunset, snow-inside-an-igloo,
snow-tears-turn-to-icicles, a snow-
a-bear-is-tracking, snow-blood-
splatters.
　　　And in Arabic also
words amounting to five-thousand-
seven-hundred-and-eighty-four steam
from the camel.
　　　As though those
and thousands crowding thousands more,
coupling night and day, could tell
the whole story!
　　　As though,
given helpmate camel and the snow,
constants through the hurly-burly
of a life, one or the other does not
become—each word precisely spoked
from it—the axis for whatever happens.

You and I have lived together
over forty years, traveled through
some twenty countries. Well, are you,
the habits, whims, minute details of,
not my weather, for one happy spell
balm jasmine breathes, the next
wind-sinewed snow?

                    The wide world
desert at an instant turned into one
baffling sandstorm, a gaunt camel
draggles me through;
                    nomadic,
driven by the windy heat, it glides
into another blinding blast, snow
exploding, covering all, a hump
among unmoving humps.
                    That camel,
thick or thin, water sloshing in it,
clumps along, with days and nights,
a drove of vultures, sheep and drivers,
jeweled oases, fat flakes whirling
off its gallop.
                    Meantime, I, tossed
hither, yon, try reining it with words
in mighty swarms, since like the Eskimo
I know no single term redoubtable enough
for anything this living-changeable,
this mixed up with our lives, as (camel
also) snow.

A Building

                    to house
these maddened times, these squalid,
brawling lives? (Happily wasps
are sizzling, all-out war
over a muddy pool.)
                    Nearby
the sea sprawls, an incurable

‹ 292 ›

complaint. Worse than gypsies we,
our path rutted far past recognition,
rove about,
                    yet like sands
tumbled, by the breezes tossing
and the sea, namelessly in one place:
rubble we pass, aimless suburbs,
ever the same.
                    Only a wren,
building its nest in our runted
catalpa tree, savors the ensolacings
of its trill (boughs once blew,
wilful leaves;
                    Brother Wood,
walking by man's side, gave fish,
fruit, songs: each season in its turn,
each day, for new youth sprung
to explore itself,
                    friskier).
But who can long abide in flaws
of man-made weather . . . one sluggish
August day, the heat like a mob
grown ugly,
                    by the Hudson's
east bank an old cow (its trail
founded this city) bloated with many
days' death; stench proclaimed
the fury of devotion.
                    Prodded
the belly, seething rose: a snarl
of eels dragged forth from the river
up the steep, miry path, to prop
the love-churned walls.

A Living Room

for Hannah Arendt and Heinrich Bleucher

> *"The past is never dead, it is not even past."*

I

These brittle pages spread before me,
letter, manuscript, should store
some fragrance, glints long gathering.
Or at least the storm which bodies,
matching, once had set.
                                    The breathing,
different, catches: passages, this one,
that, their phrases off pitch, stiff,
seem to be straining to remember.

What a time it is, this time
let out, as though I've jimmied
a closet till now hid
                            (much like
the low door I found years ago
behind some beams, a bed, a heavy
chest of drawers, in an old
Bath lodging house,
                            which opened
on, discarded with its century,
the jutting cornice of a mansion),

free within its atmosphere to be
nothing but itself, attend to nothing
but itself.

II

            There, for a moment,
like some eye considering the view
beneath its lid a world enough,

a living room.
                     And late-noon-silvered
willows which had never made it
into these pages sprinkle twilight
(mountain pines beyond already mining
the harvest moon, a mass of shimmers)
through the room.
                     As through it,
sounding out the dark, the char-
plush rustle of a train, its smoke
coiling in the trees. Or rain arrived,
an earlier version, offering glosses.

Still like words worn down, the rain
asserting shapes too distant to remark,
these pages keep their strangeness.

Possibly out of the dust collecting
a later time will fathom them.
By then the people somewhere inside
may, returning, look to one out here.

        III

One out here?
                     A grey December Princeton
morning lours like a giant shadow
that a snow, fast approaching, casts,
a train puffing along, and we lost
in it, lost inside its cloud of smoke.

Despite their bulk, in faded summer-
gaudy jackets even my stoutest volumes
flitter, while the Persian reproduction
on the wall, its light-clad figures
ruffled, flaps before the icy blasts.

‹ 295 ›

And I, pulling out a plain brown
envelope stuffed through the mail-slot,
read the name scribbled in the upper
left-hand corner,
                  name of her I saw
just yesterday at a popular Manhattan
memorial chapel, in a narrow plain
brown wooden box (just like the one
her husband filled five years before
when she whom I thought self-possessed
had riveted her gaze fast to his face).

Her packet's note transfixes me:

> "Such a terrible long time since I
> last saw you and talked with you.
> Don't you ever come to New York?
> I'm getting less and less willing
> to move. . . . take this as an excuse
> to call me."

IV

            Hannah, young vibrant muse
to Heidegger, Jasper's spiritual daughter,
German confidante and English of Jarrell,
Auden's final choice for a companion
("I came back to New York only because
of you."), Heinrich's chief, abiding lover,
gruff, imperious,
            thick smoky wreaths
ubiquitous around her blurted words,
now in the living room of their apart-
ment looking out upon the easygoing
Hudson, noon compiling ripples—

                                                quivered
like her city's spires, ancient cities
she, loving, had to leave—which echo
squealing cars and roaring buses, loose
on Riverside Drive, the last time I see her
(Heinrich, "alive in every corner and at
every moment," hovering between us) alive,

and she, finally deciding what
I long have hoped for: "Heinrich's lectures"—
the main reason for our months on months
of meeting, but foiled in each attempt
("Why it's as if that humpback imp, mischief
its chief delight, never lost sight of us!")—
"I alone must shape for publication,"

bustling over me, a proper Jewish mother,
feeds me chicken soup with dumplings!

        v

Midweek and Heinrich knocking at my door:
        "I want your book of poems at once.
        Tomorrow I am to see a publisher."
He brooking no demur, my protesting
it not finished, off it goes with him.

That Friday in New York to teach
the course that Heinrich had arranged
("You are too much a stick-in-the-mud
in Bard."), before our classes as he
nears, I see that something's happened.

        "Ted, I don't know how to tell you
        this. But when I got to New York,

‹ 297 ›

my cab dashing off, your book was gone.
Since then and with the police I have
been looking for it everywhere."

Though, beyond some printed poems
and earlier drafts, nothing remains, I,
remarking his distress, must comfort him.
The Scarlet Letter I uncover to my class
flares out livid as it's ever been.

Should I blame him, who fled the Nazis
over several countries, for enabling
through solicitude that manuscript
to join those countless other works
destroyed?
        Who then deserves my rancor?

VI

"You don't know me?
O look and see.
This crookback's my
identity.

An elf from tales
of Germany,
I've popped into
the USA.

Of your bad luck
the guardian,
if your pot breaks
by me it's done.

A miser hooked
on misery,

‹ 298 ›

when trouble strikes
and someone wails,

I am most gay,
as now when you,
too busy, fail
to notice me.

So I bestow
my dear regards.
Account your loss
my calling card."

Ah well, bowed down before this blow,
must I not also pray for that ingenious
hail-fellow?
          Who else, by cursing,
so successfully prevails on me
to trim my lines for such emergencies
and then in turn cooks up emergencies
(O ironies!) quite the reverse,

VII

as Hannah's note, continuing, reveals:

"Today going through Heinrich's papers
I found a folder with poems from you.
I hope to God you have copies.
Anyway, I'm sending it back to you
in case anything in your files
is missing.
          Warm regards.
                    Yours,
                    Hannah."

Missing? Here and now, nearly two
decades later, spread before me,
that manuscript, my book-to-be,
Outlanders, somewhere buried among
Heinrich's files!
                    His rush from train
to taxi with a pile of papers,
crookback helping, must have caused
confusion. And his mind caught up
far beyond the glut of things.

An autodidact he, admiring the pariah,
any man freestanding, that naked flute-
player, lounging, buoyant as she pipes
a meditative tune, upon her stele
on the Greek postcard he sent us.

Torn between German and English,
he, like Lao Tse at the border, customs
fronting, would declare but one short
statement which, transparent, potent,
as a water drop, must change the world.

Small wonder writing comes so hard.

    VIII

Instead Heinrich of the high places,
dapper past hope or fear and gone past
expectations of others, so accepting,
open to—at first his broad camaraderie
offended me—each one, yet hoping still,
devoted like Hannah to community,
the polis,
                    Heinrich with his thin cigars,
his thick Berliner accent, deep down

‹ 300 ›

grumbles, flash-eyed shoutings, spouting
like Vesuvius in their old world living
room amid the clash of amiable minds,

arguing, not less than with his friends
and Hannah's, with their dearest intimates,
Homer, Plato, Nietzsche, Kafka, Faulkner,
as though, everlasting in the flesh,
their minds still musing and through him
and her still making up their minds,

in the arrows he lets loose, no matter
what extremity may corner him, insouciant
since never losing sight of the bull's-eye
(he, fancying himself a military expert—
once recruited by the Kaiser's army,
had he not learned to elude the Nazis?—
his inspired, dashing troops deployed,
resorts to sallies, ambushes, raids),

addresses each Bard freshman class
as though the elders, august senators,
of Athens were assembled before him:

IX

"An artist never raises the question
directly since he cannot doubt—
as a pregnant woman, under normal
circumstances, scarcely doubts—
the value of life.
                    Yet he alone
lives this question permanently,
his whole work one emphatic answer.
The artist's impulse springs from the
initial shock that meaninglessness

is possible at all, let alone
boredom and banality;
                              this shock
provokes an immediate transcending
action, which, contradicting
the question itself, by Beauty's aura
again and again assures the artist
and the beholder that, awaiting one
bold enough to wake it, meaning exists
everywhere."

                    Several students, bemused,
then gaping, promptly slump into sleep;
others stare, incredulous at what
their ears are taking in; but a few,
like new buds thirsting, guzzle it
while Socrates, a full-time talker also
impatient of pale writing, once more,
bantering his distraught companions,
nonchalantly quaffs the bitter cup.

      "My friends, promise me, whatever happens,
      you will not contrive, and least of all
      with drugs, to rob me of my death."

(Aging, his crack troops, scattered
far afield in wind and snow, contend
with tough guerrilla bands ever more
elusive, daring, and with mutineers
as well who would join already
fighting rebels.
                    To retrieve these forces
from remote, harsh desert lands exacts
an always greater effort. And returning,
exhaustion weighs on them, the strain
of fending off a growing enemy.)

‹ 302 ›

X

But I,
hearing from Hannah and Heinrich together,
as if a stormy spell may still be coiling
through the pages of my manuscript,
shove it into a crowded drawer.

As much dare look at that crookback
chortling here, at Heinrich's lectures
stowed away on some secluded shelf.

Let them declare, like lidded lavender
the names still green and branching out
in memory, the meaning everywhere!

XI

All parts of the Olympic games,
the gods bent over, fervidly regarding?

Hannah agrees:

"One goes there for fame; another
for trade. But the best ones sit there
in the amphitheater just to look.
Only such can get the gist out of it.

So, while some are mainly interested
in doing, I am not. Looking, you see,
is what I am after. I can very well
live without doing anything. Therefore,
I get less and less willing to move.

You think me passive? A pariah
from the start, a woman and a Jew,

‹ 303 ›

I, by nature, am not an actor.
On the contrary.
                    And even when Heinrich
(after Hitler!) beat me over the head
with a hammer, waking me to the urgent,
lesser, murderous realities, I still
had this advantage: to look at the world
from the outside.
                    And now, if I would
think, I must withdraw. After hard,
long years, the world our passionate care,
have I, to shun "the they," their talk,
their trivialities, washed over every-
thing, not won the right to such retreat?

A bearing out this thinking is,
sitting here intent, speeding past
all measurement, the way that aspen
leaves sail off at any breeze.
A blessed keeping which action itself
can never fully realize.

Forgive me, but a little boredom is
quite healthy. And, so long as it is not
allowed to overwhelm our appetite
for greatness, some commonplace as well.

More than enough I've traveled,
the blurred, lurching ships and trains,
the hissing waves, the belching smoke,
the jammed-up boxcar we just missed
turning soon enough into that smoke-
bound car nothing stops, nobody misses.

So I ponder the world, its rush of strange
events, mishaps, yes, even monstrosities.

These, free as they are, unpredictable,
our storytelling proves inevitable.
I cannot live without trying every day
to understand—and never, up and down
the slippery stairs, a bannister to lean
on!—the wonder of their being, meaning.

Poetry, yours, is it so different?

Thinking, freed of physical obstacles,
for me amounts to sheer activity.
In the older Cato's words, 'When I do
nothing I am most active, and when I'm
by myself, I am the least alone.'

The moment you cannot sit still,
cannot admit plurality, the endless
dialogue between yourself and you,
contending with the world, you surely
stumble over your own feet. As Plato
said, "Your body always wants to be
taken care of and to hell with it!"

XII

And yet are we not after pleasure,
the passions, even the most painful,
pouring forth their rhapsodies as they
erupt in and through the bodied mind
out of collision with the world, lust
in the best of us for pleasure so vast
it seeks whatever excess, outrage
earth can muster?
                              Needs it—as some
plants require fiercest storms to tear
away their outer husks—and needs

‹ 305 ›

to praise, praise which, pitting itself
against the worst, sucks nectar strength
out of the wounds that tales be told,
songs sung, praise.

    XIII

              August blazing,
I spend the day with Hannah and Heinrich
in Palenville. This summer once again
they occupy a little, box-shaped cottage
to escape the city's jungle squalor and,
among the Catskills, rugged path and wake
of a volcano—
             climbing them, the jolt
of every step on rock throughout the body,
one can feel that first eruption still,
its aspiration, as it hurled itself,
voluminous fire, headlong in the heavens—

to recover from the year's packed rigors
as from our storm-beleaguered epoch,
though their windows show a village
sprawled in shacks and dumps, garages,

which confirms that they, adjusting old
familiar terrors to the foreign new
as to abasements opening on depths
still able to surprise, are still adrift
aboard the ship set sail with crew—
its passengers stroll into view—unseen,
its orders and its destination sealed.

And still they seek the sacred polis.

XIV

Inevitably talk of poetry prevails.
Another visitor, a charter member
of their tribe, hand to her brow
as if to help her understand, inquires:

    "Pray tell, how do you Americans manage?
    Never to learn by heart beloved poems
    for the dark and lonely times! Who are
    your companions then?"
                        And as I hunch
forward in that simple living room
between Hannah and Heinrich, suddenly
a unison, they chant; their phrases,
soaring
        ("Da stieg ein Baum. O reine
        Übersteigung!"),
                    smitten like their con-
centrated glances by the molten sun
descending, glitter.
              I am caught
up in the empyrean middle—a capacious
temple, perched as on a sky-capped summit,
building of that terrible, blithe marble,
only stone to last in being lava still
like bristling stars, the stately breath.

There, for a moment, in that double
sibilance, and flared as by a burning
glass, the paired-off animals draw near,
their stir, their roars, now stilled,
all ears to learn their private names,
I too—the moon already, famous with
the wind-strummed pines, allotting light—
engrossed among these numberless regards.

‹ 307 ›

XV

More than ten years past, having come
this far in the poem, I pause, dig out
the manuscript and, riffling through,
dare look at its like-coffin-browning
pages.
          Some of the poems differ
from my final versions. Others take
me, strangers, by surprise, yet promptly
for their stiff-locked cadence spring
to mind.
          At once I'm in a living
room, its windows flung wide open
to the sky, as if, someone unfolding
a letter—
               pressed inside its leaves
a tiny, faded flower, mountain laurel,
what is left of one particular morning—
morning, atop this autumn afternoon,
bursts from its pages;
                         gusts rousing
out of trees and braided with day's ric-
ochet from mountains hulked behind,
a couple dally, once more fledglings
nestled like the larks that towered round
them, rue-and-laurel-interwoven wreath.

XVI

And I not looking back, yet looking,
feeling like an ore long buried struck
or like a river as it, riding, deepens
for its travels down inside a cavern
out to sea,
          these two (have they not

‹ 308 ›

waited all this time ahead of me?) break,
sparkling, forth upon the blood's whole-
hearted tide out on this stream of notes,
a storming, my breath dares to flourish
in the dark.
        This way they look to me . . .

A Slow Fuse

Some seventy years later
your father, sitting at your table
over wine he savors, last rays mellow-
ing in it, recalls his favorite aunt,
Rifka.
        "Just naming her shoots
rifles off again inside the morning
square, rifles she aimed into the air
for certain customers, the pigeons
erupting."
        Handsome, clever,
but with little actual schooling,
she, a Jewess, kept a shop in Moscow,
stocking horse- and battle-gear,
bustling all day long.
        Powders,
braided with his laboring breath,
still prickle inside his nostrils;
like the wayward flickers cast
by lazily swimming,
        naked limbs,
leathers polished, buckles, gleam;
and the oats banked in their bins,

heavy August winds drowsed in them,
at one glance, a single sniffing,
bloom;
       the harnesses and bells,
by gaslight starred, send out appeals,
while sleighs collect for midnight
junkets.
       He smitten with it all,
like those officers of the Czar
who, admiring her wit, her seasoned
gaiety, forever jammed the shop.

"Even the city's metropolitan,
young despite his full, black robes,
took to dropping in on her, his jagged,
bushy beard awag with chat.
       One balmy
summer evening, I remember, the three
of us, laughter brimming like wine
(he turned his glass to the lessened
light), relaxed in her snug flat.

The next morning at breakfast,
talk going on as if we'd never stop"—
he, a startled look lit on his face,
breaking in upon himself, exclaims,
the pigeons crackling through the air—
"My God, he spent the night with her!"

He, sipping the last drop, sits
back, as much as he's amazed amused
to see this special virtue of old age,
the oats ripening only in slow time.

A Pair of Shoes

This, you were sure, whatever happened,
you'd remember, long as any thought
stuck in your head.
                              After a bitter
winter, when you and your family had
to eat weeds, bark, scraps of leather,
and it seemed certain the caked ice
would last forever,
                              the first lull came
drifting over. And then, more sudden
than the dusk invading, a tattered army,
raping, looting, killed all the others,
burned down the huts, and disappeared
before the smoke could scatter.
                              This
you were sure you'd remember, the blood
of your mother soaked in your blouse.

That was how many epochs, how many
countries, earthquakes, holocausts ago?
And oceans washing through, the cloudy
dreams, how many furnished rooms, a rusty
stain on them from how many people?

Now you are old and bent over, old
and bent to this spot called New York.
And crossing the street, only one thing
matters: to keep these broken shoes,
three sizes too big, from falling off.

Beside such chore, your left foot
slowly, slowly sliding after the other,
what a far-off, pointless tale that memory.

‹ 311 ›

Let those sporting a polished pair
which fit indulge themselves.
                              Crossing
this street, the weight of you collected,
the old blood shuffles through your veins,
too busy to remember.

The Place of Laughter

In some countries laughter
is forbidden, a luxury, a kind
of sin, belonging to the mindless
or the mad.
                So for one poet
"the man who laughs/Has simply
not yet heard the terrible news."
In other countries
                        it persists
almost apart from circumstances,
fruits without a tree, laughter
at—if not
                out of—extremities.
However, in the villages of India,
at least as you observed them,
if the people
                stay alive, they,
burnished by hard times, famine,
plagues, trying all their strength,
shine out like deities,
                        women,
heavy bundles balanced like crowns,

erectly walking, with a laughter
rarely heard
             but weaving
through their bodies' movements
and their glances soft if piercing,
the way trees stand,
                welcoming
winter, easing sun-stricken summer
with leaves that seem to listen
as they wave,
            shadowy laughter.
Or that little flower breaking out
from a seed that's had to push
its way through granite.

The Here and Now

for Yehuda Amichai

Though you live in a little country,
crammed and crisscrossed with debris,
the past oppressive many times over—
where you buy your grapes David, pausing,
eyes a fiery dark girl, a lusty song
riding his breath, the old dance urgent
at his body; where you buy your bread
Christ, stumbling, stoops to heavy lumber—
you insist on your own loves and griefs,
on living your own life.
                So you love
this city, but mainly as it goes on
living its own life, across its roofs

the lines flapping, not gaudy banners,
but sheets and diapers, pants and slips,
as if rehearsing private pleasures.

And though you know you cannot win,
you play the game with all the skill
and love that you can muster, hoping
to keep it, keep it going, whatever
the fierceness in it, while you learn
the repertoire of your opponent's wrist,
the repertoire your own commands,
with every stroke surprising you,
as in a woman's glance the abundance
glinting of her passion stored away.

Those opposing roles, victor, victim
both, when they require re-enacting,
the moon as ever plays the luminous dome
above your god-and-man-scarred rock,
responsive to each nuance of the light
informing it with this, the latest scene.

The sweat you've shared between you,
juices drying on your hands and moon-
lit belly, swirls out of the rutted, stain-
stiff sheets a fragrance stronger, more
anointing, than the myrrh, the frank-
incense the magi brought, a gleam
that would eclipse their beaten gold.

Making It

(Jerusalem, July 4, 1980)

Easily as the moon
comes,
     as surprising . . .

    I

the eyes rising
to the shining surface
of this violin
         you rented:
its old wood, newly
carved,
     is redolent
still to nose and finger,

the body a big, curving
sound . . .

    II

        and the stone
of this city, ages ground
in ages,
     the unblemished
sunlight, daylong trooping
days
     sunk into it,

but pink & yellow flowers
welling out of it,
crowns in little like

the moon now over it,
as though newly polished,
newly made . . .

    III

make it new,
make it now,
make it . . .

    IV

        the scrawny
young black cat, that
fixed us
        through a window
of our room with her
triangular
        Egyptian stare,
already several times
a mother
        with all her
skittish, half-crazed, little
kittens,

    V

        crouches in the
doorway, shadow-silent,
waiting
        for the geckos,
prehistoric mini-monsters,
scarabs of good luck,

which, once dusk arrives,
out hunting, skitter

across
      our outdoor wall,
the chittering their name,
one with the voices
              laden
in the air, making it,
here in Israel . . .

    VI

only appetite, that cat's,
the geckos', ancient
as the moon,
          its latest
luster that predates those
hoary rocks,
        like you and me,
the old gods throbbing
in us,
     the looks flocked
from your fingers, penetrant
as any star,
        only the song,
risen like a wellspring
from this violin,
         out
of the prayers, the bloody
sighs, the wailing,
          easily
as the moon comes,
its luminous calm, ever

    making it new,
    making it now,
    making it . . .

The Death of Fathers

Rummaging inside yourself
for clues and coming up
with nothing more than old
familiar news, you think
you have it hard.
      Your
father having died when you
were still a child, you keep,
it's true, but faded sense
of him.
    Soon after that,
as though to make it worse,
the village he was born
and lived in all his life
dispersed.
    And now—
perhaps with him it joined
the lost tribes of Virginia—
it survives, name only,
on discarded, browning maps.

But though my father died
when I was some years older,
I know, beyond all ordinary
disappearings, nothing
of his past, his country

(Hungary he called it,
only a few of his oaths
still peppery on my tongue
to prove it), least of all
his town.
    New vandals

‹ 318 ›

rampant, kicking boundaries
askew, whole nations also
on the run, as though their
lands were made of wind-

blown sand, how expect
to know? (Only when, Hitler
bringing my father's country
home to him, the two of us
hunched
        by the radio,
did I get a bitter sense
of who my father might have
been and was and of his
world
        in a past much
overlaid.) Like you I try
to ferret out whatever hints
of him from the one source
still available—myself.

Recall a few of his
loved saws like "The apple
never falls far from its tree."
But only a worm in it sticks
its fat tongue out at me.

Or "Teddy, I understand
you all right. Are you not
my son?" Well, was he not
my father? Clues or not,
chasing fast scribbled lines,

I lean on his robustious
love: his skill with animals:
his joy in gypsy fiddling,

‹ 319 ›

notes ripening within his
fingers' will: his passion

for his work, I awed
watching him—old things
bought, and new, to sell—
danced among green filing-
cabinets, as he, a boy,

shoes riding his neck,
had skipped along (he told
me this?) the speckled path
bisecting the Black Forest:
pride that almost drove

him, raging, over cliffs
and finally, when, despite
strong warnings, he would
mount a frisky horse, rode
him off forever,
     I there
by him as he stumbles up,
eyes closed, face set,
a name, my mother's,
still hot upon his lips.

And gripping his arm,
I summon all my strength
("Am I not your son?"
Surely I can reach him,
haul him back), to learn—

as I shout "Father!"
over the growing chasm,
his breath slammed shut,
a wall instantly gone up—
the lesson never learned.

The Hostage

The young man, all mixed up,
long before he used it dumped
his life to take on something
else because it sounded, if not
better, different.
                So he landed
in jail for assorted crimes,
in a country he couldn't name.
Little more than a pail he had
to remind him
              what his days
were coming to, and a straw cot
so hard, so narrow, it failed
to bear him and his dreams.
These anyway grew
             so fat
that they, his sleep unable
to accommodate the least of them,
the cell too small, promptly
overran his days.
            Until a fly
flew in and, lounging back,
seemed to ponder him.
              Returning,
pondered day by day.
             And sleep
began to work: the fly, at first
with wings and then without,
then wings, free of the body,
always bigger
           as they flapped,
flew—cell shaking like a storm-
struck ship—him out into the open
air beyond the need of wings

until he woke.
                    Whatever fly
smuggled in of plums it had sipped,
lips it had briefly perched upon,
and choice pollution, it denied
to sit and ponder him.
                    Grown fond
of it, he, catching it, tore off
its wings to keep it, hardly
worse off than he.
                    Appreciation,
which made his loneliness less,
made this possible.
                    Between them,
needing little, they managed
a world. What's more, he could
afford to feed it fabulously.

Earthrise

Like the conquistadors
our moon men lusted after novelty,
world out of this world no one
had ever visited before?

Every second passing,
though it seem a commonplace,
pries some unexpected door. Every
second a stepping into the unknown,

a leaping in the mind
that the breath catches, the heart

in its sputtering flame matches
against the delicious fear.

Moon more than enough
this body, this whirligig star
we wander, heaven enough the space
our looks dart through,

our talk: earth flies
with us, swamps and mountains,
eagles peaking, snow-packed clouds,
the rivers pouring over,

cataracts. And burrowed
far below, those furry meteors
of the mineral dark: mole sedulous
with sidekick squeaky bat

and mouse. Those also,
bearded comets, sparks struck
off, fellow travelers streaming by,
like us equipped to people

briefly our atmosphere.
Last night the fireflies composed
a galaxy, a complex universe,
among the trees. Falling

together mouth to mouth,
the dark, its planets, backing us,
we sighed forth air unhusked
a god might yearn to use.

Moon on our hands
and everywhere, space fell
away. For the rapture whirling us
a song too close to hear.

❖ ❖ ◆ ❖ ❖

FROM

From Princeton One Autumn Afternoon

«1987»

❖ ❖ ◆ ❖ ❖

From Princeton one autumn afternoon, 1986

I

Dear Zbigniew Herbert,

Someone said all poems compose
one poem. Who's to judge him wrong?
Have I not long been occupied
with speculations having to do
with those in your "The Old Masters?"

So, while our fall is at its peak,
trees galleries jammed with jostling
masterpieces, I, though we've
not met, feel called upon to write
to you.
　　　Because they never thought
to autograph their work, you,
envious, urge those Old Masters

　　make the serpent scales of pride
　　fall from me

　　let me be deaf
　　to the siren calls of fame

‹ 327 ›

II

Could you and I believe the God
we aimed to please was watching, angels
too, fluttered over angels we had
newly hatched, we'd also slight
our names.
            But if these works are real,
their angels, their events, the light
they shed secure in each, why should
they need to be identified?

Once it's done a great painting seems
to have produced itself and waits
on us, orphans that we are, to claim,
proclaim it and so name ourselves.

Even now we can appreciate
what miracle those works achieve,
each one a meeting (mating) place
for heaven and earth their makers,
making, slipt into.
            As you say,

    uttering no frightened cry
    no plea to be remembered
    they drowned without a trace
    in golden firmaments

III

And even here and now like them
I'd press this gallant bustle—
trillion bushes burning, burning
babes in rushes, crucifixions

‹ 328 ›

by the bushel dangled from sumacs,
maples, sycamores—between my pages.

Gladly too I'd drown in it.

This windfall should remind us of
many a painting's sky-borne company.
Incarnation of the local light,
they match up with the amber of
a roisterous beer, an auburn glance,
hair in a rush, a flashing thigh;

their flying up and down inside
the landscape seems to flourish it
forth.
      Among the candle-flickering
saints highnoon itself is caught.
Or else, as now, sunset's draining
out of clouds and banked-up foliage.

    xxx

            But as the newest
critics tell us, it's a mistake,
if not a downright fake, to think
a work, whether it be painting,
poem, song, belongs to anyone.
By godly language alone it's done.

And anyway would a rose or one
of these accomplished leaves be rosier
were it, beyond its own intricacy,
like a curled-up scroll, a painting,
proudly, plainly signed by its maker?

In any case, I judge the Old Masters
lucky because they knew the only
certain fame wholehearted striding—
sumac-, maple-, sycamore-wise—
barefoot into glory,
                    instantly
immortal, in their name-free works.

                    Yours,
                Theodore Weiss